HOW TO BUILD A WINNING COMPANY CULTURE

HOW TO BUILD A WINNING COMPANY CULTURE

Dr. Michelle Rozen

Copyright © 2016 Dr. Michelle Rozen
All rights reserved.

ISBN-13: 9781537791944
ISBN-10: 153779194X

To my beloved father, the artist of organizational culture and human interaction.

Table of Contents

Introduction: How This Book Can Help Your Company xiii

Chapter 1 Why Workplace Culture Matters So Much 1
The Seven Characteristics of Descending Company Cultures 1
   Decreased productivity 1
      Deliberate withholding of information: 2
      Lack of support to other departments and teams when needed: 2
      Gossip and bad vibes: 2
   Decreased ability to handle competition 3
   Decreased engagement 3
      Inspiration 4
      Confidence 4
      Empowerment 4
      Enthusiasm 4
   Employee turnover 5

- Unhealthy confrontation · 5
- Low morale · 6
- Frustration, anxiety, and depression · · · · · · · · · · · · · · · · 6
  - The Cost of Turnover · 8
  - Difficulties in Organizations · 8
  - Time Wasted · 8
  - Missed Days at Work · 8
  - Stress · 9
  - Depression · 9
  - On Leaders Stepping In · 9
- The Seven Characteristics of Ascending Company Cultures · 11
  - A purpose-driven company culture · · · · · · · · · · · · · · · · · 11
  - Effective communication patterns · · · · · · · · · · · · · · · · 12
  - A culture of feedback · 13
  - Embracing diversity · 14
  - Teamwork · 14
  - Engagement and loyalty · 15
  - Growth and development · 16
    - Position-based growth · 16
    - Professional growth · 17
    - Financial growth · 17
- Chapter 2   What Causes Company Cultures to Become Descending Rather Than Ascending? · 18
  - Change · 18
    - Low Clarity of Scope of Work and Policies · · · · · · · · · · 21

Adverse Personality Types · 22
  Type A Personality: · 23
  Type B Personality: · 23
  Type C Personality: · 24
  Type D Personality: · 25
Harmful Communication Patterns · · · · · · · · · · · · · · · · 25
  Poorly Expressed Messages · 27
  Assumptions · 27
  Body Language · 28
  Lack of Attention · 28
  Lack of Trust · 28
  Lack of Proper Incentive · 29
Chapter 3 How to Create an Ascending Company
Culture, Part I: Creating a Company Culture of FACT · · · 30
  Developing a Company Culture of Feedback · · · · · · · 31
  What Creates a Culture of Feedback within
  Companies? · 35
  Promoting a Company Culture of Adaptability · · · · · 36
  Embrace Change—There Is an Opportunity within It · · 36
  Fostering a Company Culture of Communication · · · 37
  Important Advantages · 38
  Encouraging a Company Culture of Teamwork · · · · · 43
  Benefits of Teamwork · 44
  Team Characteristics · 45
  The Two Most Common Problems When It
  Comes to Teamwork: · 48

Chapter 4 How to Create an Ascending Company Culture, Part II: Soaring to New Heights with the Red-Shift Blue-Shift Model · 50
   Red-Shift Actions and Their Impact on Company Culture · 51
      Unleash Attack · 52
      Recruit Pack · 54
      Guard Territory · 56
      Exercise Self-Defense · 56
   Categorizing Red-Shift Dynamics · · · · · · · · · · · · · · · · · · 58
      Tunnel Vision · 58
      Assuming vs. Courageous Conversations · · · · · · · · · · 82
      The One-Solution Approach vs. the Multiple-Solutions Approach · 96
   The Best Trick for Bringing Opposing Team Members Together · 102
   How to Externalize the Problem that Led to the Conflict · 105
      1. Separate the person from the problem. · · · · · · · · · · 105
      2. Personify the problem and attribute oppressive intentions and tactics to it. · · · · · · · · · · · · · 106
   Benefits of externalizing the problem: · · · · · · · · · · · · · 106
   Defusing Bombs · 107
      1. Timing · 109
      2. Empathy · 109
      3. Externalization · 109
      4. Collaboration · 110

Chapter 5   A Few Words of Summary · · · · · · · · · · · · · · · · 111
Chapter 6   Test Yourself: Does Your Company
Demonstrate Characteristics of an Ascending Company
Culture or a Descending Company Culture? · · · · · · · · · · · 113

Works Consulted · 117

Introduction: How This Book Can Help Your Company

The goal of enhancing company culture should be at the heart of every organization. We often see a company's culture as its personality, and as a result, it really determines how the company operates. That culture, then, is essential to the success of the company as well as to its ability to grow within its market, sustain and increase its growth, handle competition well, and overcome obstacles and challenges. Company culture should never be neglected, and it should be cultivated on an ongoing basis. So how can this book help your company? Well that's simple: by showing you how you can enhance the culture of your own company.

You may be asking what this term "culture" means and whether your company already has one. Well, the answer is yes, your company already has its own culture. In fact, every organization, from the smallest business to the largest corporation, has a culture. "Culture" refers to the values and attitudes of the employees within the business. Naturally, not all cultures are the same, and there are even different types of culture. In this book, we differentiate between cultures that are on the rise and those that are not—ascending company cultures and descending company cultures.

In descending company cultures, employees act as individuals and perform their duties to meet their own needs, such as a paycheck or health insurance. In these types of cultures, there is a high level of employee turnover; employees tend to have a lower morale and a lower level of engagement, and they struggle when it comes to teamwork and productivity. That in turn affects customer service and ultimately damages the sales and profitability of the company.

Ascending company cultures, on the other hand, give value to each employee in the organization. Of course these employees care about their own advancement as in descending cultures, but they also work as a team to meet the goals of the company and benefit its customers. Teamwork is important in these types of cultures, morale and engagement are high, and employee retention is good. Employees work as a team to increase sales, provide the best customer service, and advance the company's goals in any way possible.

So Where Do You Stand?

In reality, most companies are somewhere in the middle. Their teamwork is OK but could be improved. Engagement is acceptable but should be worked on, and so on. They are ascending in some ways and descending in others, and so company culture needs to be enhanced.

One thing that is important to remember, though, is that the enhancement of company culture is an ongoing process. Yes, the impact of challenges is cumulative and can be devastating in the long term, but once an ascending company culture is reached and maintained, the company can truly achieve new heights of growth and success.

This book, then, will teach you not only *why* it matters but also *how* to achieve that ascending-culture status. It won't change your company completely, because enhancement of company culture builds on the strengths that are already there, but it will bring an awareness of any leaks and squeaks in engagement, teamwork, and productivity. With the help of this book, you'll be able to analyze the source of any issues and put practical tools in place to enhance your company's culture. As a result, you and your company will be better, bigger, stronger, and most definitely more successful.

1

Why Workplace Culture Matters So Much

So I've established in the introduction that workplace culture is important and that there are two main types of company culture: ascending company culture and descending company culture. Each type has seven defining characteristics. In this chapter, I'll examine each of those characteristics individually.

THE SEVEN CHARACTERISTICS OF DESCENDING COMPANY CULTURES

Decreased productivity

Descending company cultures are conflict saturated, which has a direct and devastating impact on productivity and the success of the company overall. How can employees focus on work and be at their peak performance if they go to work every day worried and preoccupied with the conflicts they are experiencing in the workplace? The answer is they can't. These conflicts hurt their focus, their time management, and definitely their ability to be at their best. So before they even begin work, this heated and disturbing workplace environment causes employees to produce a lot less than their capabilities and a lot less than their previous performance.

It's not just about individuals, though. Teams are affected too, as they are unable to function at their best in a conflict-saturated environment. This typically comes into play in three major ways.

Deliberate withholding of information:
This is where teams or departments either deliberately withhold information from each other or just refrain from sharing because they prefer not to communicate. This directly hurts company productivity, customer service, and the ability to come up with new products and ideas.

Lack of support to other departments and teams when needed:
If there is conflict within or between teams of workers, they are less likely to help each other. The general sense in those cases is, why help the enemy? Teams will allow their rivals to suffer in the hope that management will see how incapable they are and in order to show management what the team has to deal with every day.

Gossip and bad vibes:
Workplace gossip can take much time and energy, and it can keep employees away from their real tasks for long periods over a given workweek.

Decreased ability to handle competition

If there is one way to beat your opponents in an increasingly competitive market, it's by having teams and departments that are united and working at their best. When teams don't work well together, their work performance suffers, and as a result, the competition will have the upper hand. After all, they are busy producing rather than fighting and dealing with bad vibes.

It's important to remember that this is not something that *might* happen. It is just a question of time. If you have a descending company culture, competitors in an ascending company culture will always have the upper hand.

Decreased engagement

A descending company culture typically manifests itself pretty quickly through decreased employee engagement and a low level of motivation overall. Engagement is a key component to the company's productivity and success, and it typically relies on four key sources.

- Relationship with direct manager
- Relationship with team/department members
- Trust in management overall
- Pride in working for the company

Without a positive company culture, employees are less likely to engage, and that is ultimately negative for your organization.

Truly engaged employees are an asset to every company and would typically demonstrate four major traits. I call them the ICEE Traits of the Engaged Employee.

Inspiration
Engaged employees feel inspired by their superiors and team members as well as by their work environment.

Confidence
Engaged employees are confident in their own ability to produce, succeed, and reach their goals. They are also confident that their work environment supports their efforts and helps them in any possible way, for the benefit of the company.

Empowerment
Engaged employees feel empowered by their management and by the power of their positions to create, solve problems, and push things forward. They feel empowered by the trust, appreciation, and faith that the management has in them.

Enthusiasm
Engaged employees are enthusiastic about what they do at work. They feel valuable and validated, and they are excited to contribute and push things forward for the company.

Employee turnover

A conflict-saturated company culture is an unhealthy environment to work in, and so employee turnover tends to be high. Nobody likes to go to work every day having to deal with conflict, frustration, and anxiety. Often, then, this causes a company's best employees to seek other work options. After all, if you can work in a positive environment rather than a negative one,  why wouldn't you? This often happens right under the radar of management and team leaders who may not be fully aware of just how much a descending company culture impacts the employee.

Unhealthy confrontation

Confrontation is not necessarily a negative thing, and it can often serve the purpose of productivity and success when handled respectfully and in a proactive manner. A healthy confrontation like this leads to a productive dialogue. It doesn't always happen like that, though, and problems occur when people hold grudges and experience anxious and negative feelings. When this happens, people may confront others in an unexpected, angry manner. This as an unhealthy confrontation, and it could lead to further anger and distance. In this sense, the confrontation doesn't promote the two sides' interests, collaboration, and teamwork, and this will ultimately have an effect on workplace productivity.

Low morale

Descending company cultures are characterized by low morale. Employees feel bad about themselves and about their environment, and they have an ongoing sense of being in an emotionally draining situation. The anger, sadness, sense of helplessness, anxiety, and frustration experienced in descending company cultures will directly impact the overall morale. As a result, salespeople will sell less, and producers will produce less. This is not because they mean to, of course, but because they are drained and upset. This is directly hurting company performance on various levels.

Frustration, anxiety, and depression

A descending company culture will also lead to increased frustration, anxiety, and some level of depression, depending on the severity of the situation and on the personalities of the people involved. Frustration tends to manifest itself as a result of employees' inability to do the things that are expected of them at the level that they want to do it. This might be because they can't collaborate (or at least, they can't collaborate well) with the person or persons with whom they have issues. This lack of collaboration could mean that the their rivals within the company won't share information with them in a timely manner or may not help them in the way that they should, and so, in the employees' perception at least, these "rivals" hinder their ability to perform their tasks and reach their goals in the way they would like to.

Anxiety typically stems from that frustration. Since tasks are not completed in the way that they should be and because goals are not reached, people start fearing for the security of their position one way or another. Employees in a descending company culture don't have confidence that teams members will work together toward joint goals, and they may feel other team members are weighing them down. Because of this, anxiety levels increase. Imagine trying to run forward with one leg tied to a heavy weight. Wouldn't you be anxious about still reaching your goal?

> **Typical Scenario:**
>
> **David:** I keep looking at other available positions within my field. My problems with Michael cause me so much stress; I don't think I can handle it anymore.
>
> **Dan:** Have you tried addressing it with him? Maybe I should have a word with him?
>
> **David:** Well, good luck trying. He is impossible to deal with. This is so frustrating because I cannot get my work done as long as I have someone like that in my team.
>
> **Dan:** Have you tried discussing it with management?
>
> **David:** There is no point, management will definitely put the blame on me. This is hopeless. This is really very frustrating.

Let's look at some workplace statistics that demonstrate the cost of turnover, loss of productivity, and absenteeism—in short, the cost of a descending company culture.

The Cost of Turnover
Ernst & Young reports that the cost of losing and replacing an employee may be as high as 150 percent of the departing employee's annual salary (*workforce.com*). Let's not forget that the cost of turnover also includes the manager's time in training new employees.

Difficulties in Organizations
Research shows that 60–80 percent of all difficulties in organizations come from strained relationships between employees, not from deficits in an individual employee's skill or motivation.

Time Wasted
The typical manager spends 25–40 percent of his or her time dealing with workplace conflicts. That's one to two days of work, every single week.

Missed Days at Work
Two-thirds of both men and women say work has a significant impact on their stress level, and one in four has called in sick or taken a mental-health day as a result of work-related stress.

Stress

One-fourth of employees view their jobs as the number-one stressor in their lives. Workplace stress causes approximately one million US employees to miss work each day.

Depression

American employees used about 8.8 million sick days in 2001 due to untreated or mistreated depression.

On Leaders Stepping In

Allowing employees to work out mild conflicts is a great way to build team morale and save management time, but there are situations that need more attention. In descending company cultures, leadership needs to intervene if issues become serious or are extended over time. In essence, leadership should step in if any of the following are observed:

- A sudden change in employee behavior
- A sudden change in employee body language or verbal tone
- Increased absences
- A noticeable reduction in productivity
- Noticeably increased stress levels

Once one or more of these behaviors are observed, all that's left for management is to work out what to do about it—and that is often the hardest part!

There are lots of reasons to address a culture that has begun to descend, and perhaps the most fundamental benefit is the opportunity an organization gets to learn about itself. This can help you not only function better going forward by preventing such situations from happening again, but it can also improve your overall functioning and productivity.

THE SEVEN CHARACTERISTICS OF ASCENDING COMPANY CULTURES

Ascending company cultures manifest seven distinct characteristics as well. These are company cultures that indicate growth and an upward dynamic, and they are typically characterized by a high level of teamwork and engagement. Here are the seven characteristics of ascending company cultures.

A purpose-driven company culture

Ascending company cultures are company cultures in which employees have a clear sense of purpose; employees understand their immediate and long term goals. This is important, because an organization with purpose shifts people and resources forward in order to achieve goals rather than simply managing them, and achieving goals is what it's all about, isn't it? So purpose is a key ingredient for a strong, sustainable, scalable organizational culture.

It's more than that, though. Purpose is an inspirational driver for engaging employees and communities. When a leader establishes a clear purpose for the organization, it will become the inspirational driver for engaging employees and so provide them with a concrete source for motivation. In other words, the organization's strategies, capabilities, and culture become the engine behind the organization's purpose.

What's more, the connection between purpose and performance is clear. There's mounting evidence that aligning an organization with a higher purpose drives business results. A

2014 study by Deloitte found that an organization that focuses on purpose is an organization that inspires higher levels of confidence among stakeholders and one that boosts growth. Similarly, a 2010 Burson-Marsteller/IMD Corporate Purpose Impact study found that a strong and well-communicated corporate purpose can contribute up to 17 percent improvement in financial performance. And that's just in the short term. The longer-term benefits of having employees aligned with a strong sense of purpose are incalculable.

Effective communication patterns

Effective communication patterns within ascending organizations have three main characteristics: clarity, courtesy, and proactivity.

Clarity is a vital element in effective communication, because it's important for messages and information to be transferred in a transparent, clear, and concise manner. This is true regardless of where the messages com: managers to employees or within teams. It's the clarity of these messages that allows them to be heard and processed by the receiver—and that makes clarity invaluable! Often, people don't communicate their messages clearly enough, because they are afraid of upsetting people. They may be afraid to say what they really want to say, or they dance around the actual message, hoping to get avoid saying what they actually want to say. In organizations where employees express themselves clearly and safely, teams work together better, and productivity is increased as a result.

Courtesy is another important aspect of communication, as it allows for messages to be transmitted within an atmosphere of safety and respect. It manifests respect for the other person and gets the message across within the safe limits of that respect. In this way, feedback, information, and messages can be transferred with minimal concern for getting hurt or hurting others.

Proactivity is a yet another crucial aspect of an effective communication pattern, because the only way to conduct a productive discussion is to conduct a proactive one. In real terms, this means that all parties in the discussion are forward looking rather than engaging with the past, which leads to blame and accusations. A forward-looking discussion is based on the notion that whatever happened has happened, and it can't be changed, so the discussion is more centered on what we can do from this point going forward in order to reach our goals or operate better as a team.

A culture of feedback

Feedback is great for so many reasons, and fostering a culture of feedback is crucial to the success of every organization. Why? Because feedback pushes higher levels of performance. Creating an open, feedback-oriented company culture requires people to be receptive to giving *and* receiving feedback and to understanding when and how to give it. Feedback can come from many different people and places. These people or places could be internal or external, and the feedback could be about any aspect of organizational life, including leadership and vision, management and internal practices, and operations. A culture of feedback means not only that feedback is given and received but that it is given and received safely, clearly, and productively, with sensitivity to diversity of cultures, personalities, and situations.

Embracing diversity

Cultural sensitivity is the awareness of practices and cultures that are different from your own. A culture that embraces diversity has an awareness of different cultures, of how these cultures should be properly approached, and how to communicate with them accordingly. Leaders and team members evaluate how certain cultural differences affect how people work, communicate, and interact without judging, making assumptions, discriminating, or stereotyping.

A company culture that embraces diversity is centered on tolerance and acceptance of others, which fosters teamwork and a general sense of collaboration.

Teamwork

Creating, enhancing, and celebrating teamwork is at the heart of every ascending company culture. A culture of teamwork focuses on team accomplishments rather than on individual accomplishments, encourages collaboration, and allows for tasks to be completed in a faster, better, and more efficient manner. One of the most common misconceptions about teamwork is that the success of

a team is based on the personalities of the team members. The truth is that while personalities that work well together certainly make teamwork easier, the real success or failure of teamwork is derived from structure. Teams need to know what the expectations are and what the roles and rules are. Those need to be reinforced and clarified to all team members, and once this structure is in place, teamwork becomes much easier.

Engagement and loyalty

Employee engagement is a hot topic at the moment, and raising employee engagement has become one of the highest priorities for organizations around the world. The problem is that while leaders have come to appreciate the importance of having a fully engaged employee, they often have a very limited understanding of what really drives employee engagement and of how to actually maintain or even increase it. In the 1990s, William Kahn, professor of organizational behavior at Boston University, introduced the term "engagement" based on his observation that people have a choice as to how much of themselves they're willing to invest in their jobs. Kahn discovered that employees were far more emotionally and physically engaged when they experienced the following:

- Psychological meaningfulness: a sense that their work was worthwhile and made a difference.
- Psychological safety: a feeling they were valued, accepted, respected, and able to perform their job in a positive work environment.

- Availability: routinely feeling secure and self-confident in terms of their ability to perform their job.

Nearly twenty-five years later, these three elements remain at the heart of most theories of employee engagement. The most interesting fact as far as engagement is concerned is that pay isn't even on the list! While fair compensation will always be a key component of job satisfaction, the research shows us that it's not necessarily a day-to-day motivator of engagement. The conclusion for organizations everywhere is this:

Employee engagement can never be bought; it must be earned.

Growth and development

Ascending company cultures always offer their employees opportunities for growth, both in terms of training and in terms of their ability to grow as individuals or as teams—acquiring new skills and, as a result, new possibilities. It's the manager's job not only to obtain the best possible performance from employees but to obtain the best possible performance from them while at the same time helping them to grow. Opportunities for growth are an incredibly determining factor in employee engagement, and there are various types of growth opportunities that companies can offer employees.

Position-based growth

Motivated people who work hard would typically expect to move forward and upward in terms of their position. If they do not see any possibility for position-based growth at any point, it may decrease their engagement, and in some cases it may cause them to leave.

Professional growth
Engaged and motivated employees would also seek the opportunity to enhance their skills and improve their knowledge. People desire to feel that they are progressing as professionals and that their workplace allows for that growth.

Financial growth
Financial growth is important to employees, as it can act as an indicator of their value and worth to the company. Lack of financial growth is perceived by employees as lack of growth in terms of their own value for the company, which may lead to disengagement and even increased staff turnover.

> **Dr. Rozen Says:**
> Ascending company cultures are characterized by being purpose driven and by having effective communication patterns, a culture of feedback, enhanced diversity, teamwork, engagement and loyalty, and growth and development.

2

What Causes Company Cultures to Become Descending Rather Than Ascending?

No one wants the company culture to descend, but it happens. So what causes it? The reality is that there are many factors. To explain the causes of a descending company culture, let's use what I call the CLASH model. CLASH stands for change, low clarity, adverse personality types, styles, and harmful communication.

Change

Change can have a major effect on any organization, and the modern workplace can link significant levels of stress and conflict to changes in management or staffing. Technological change can cause conflict too, as can changing work methodologies. These changes could come in the form of a new boss who has new ideas and different workflows. Even without a new boss, though, reorganization alone can lead to tremendous amounts of stress and conflict—and the rate of reorganization in some workplaces is almost chronic! Leadership may be about change, but change causes anxiety to many, and nothing is worse for productivity than extreme and disturbing anxiety in the workplace. Instead of focusing on their own productivity or the success of the company overall, employees will focus on their sources of anxiety (job loss, loss of power, loss of advantages, and so on), and that will ultimately have a negative effect on the organization as a whole.

One of the reasons that change has such a negative effect is that it interferes with autonomy, and that can make people feel that they've lost control over their territory and their power. It also creates uncertainty, and if change feels extremely uncertain, then people will reject it. People will often prefer to remain in misery than to head toward an unknown. In life in general, as much as in the workplace, we all need a sense of safety. With change, many unknowns create much irritability.

This uncertainty can mean that any decisions that are imposed suddenly on people may cause them anxiety and distress. In these cases, everything seems different. Routine, as much as it is often complained about, brings certainty and confidence to many, so decisions that seem sudden or rash can create much bitterness and talk in the hallways.

Change can result in other misgivings, too. In departing from the past and moving toward newer regulations, many will worry about loss of respect, face, and status. One example of this could be a lack of skill or knowledge that was perhaps protected or hidden by older regulations, and an employee may fear that these inadequacies or incompatibilities are about to be exposed. Similarly, change also brings concerns of being able to adapt to the new requirements. This is especially true with technology. Those that are not as technologically savvy may take longer to learn new systems and feel extremely intimidated and agitated. Many will also worry that more will be required of them once the new changes are in place, and they are not sure how to meet those requirements.

All of these issues can cause resentment, which will come in two major forms: past resentment and present resentment. Past resentment is sometimes hidden away and kept quiet while everything is steady, but once change occurs and anxiety increases, these old resentments may surface again—and the older they are, the harder they may be to resolve. New resentment, on the other hand, stems from the newly created circumstances, and they often occur when older employees feel threatened by the newer arrivals and feel that their knowledge and experience are either not currently valued or may not be valued in the future.

The threat of change and the anxiety it causes are more than understandable. Change is promising to some, and perhaps vital to the organization, but it's dangerous to others. Because of that, change requires proactive conflict-management practices. In other words, management need to prevent conflict before it escalates. The Red-Shift Blue-Shift model, which we will talk about in greater detail later on, aims to do exactly that. This model assists organizations in creating a language of effective conflict management throughout the organization during times of change or turmoil, in order to proactively address conflicts when they are still small, to increase engagement, and to create a company culture of true teamwork.

Low Clarity of Scope of Work and Policies

There is no difference between bigger and smaller corporations when it comes to low levels of clarity in terms of the scope of employees' work or company policies. Regardless of the size of your organization, a lack of clarity will always lead to conflict. The rule of thumb when it comes to employees' scope of work and to company policies is "detail, detail, detail." Detail aids clarity. In every situation where things are defined in a vague or partially vague manner, messages are open not only to interpretation but also to negotiation and power struggles. This isn't because employees are necessarily trying to allocate more power to themselves (which may very well be the case, but it's not always) but because employees may truly make different assumptions as far as the scope of their work goes, what the policies are, and what is expected of them. When their perceptions of expectations, scope, and policies clash, they will interpret that clash in a personal manner, and conflict becomes inevitable. After all, when employees are unsure of what is expected of them, how can they be expected to perform in the best possible way? They can't, and that is why detail and clarity are so important.

> **Typical Scenario:**
>
> **Elaine:** I talked to that client that called yesterday, and Rich got very mad at me.
>
> **Linda:** Really? How come?
>
> **Elaine:** Well, Rich thought that answering client inquiries is something that Sales needs to handle but when John was the manager, Operations could take calls from clients as well, if no one from Sales was around to take the call.
>
> **Linda:** I'm so confused. Why was Rich mad? Did anyone ever announce that there is a new policy as far as taking calls from clients?
>
> **Elaine:** No. This is what is so confusing about it.
>
> **Linda:** If they want us to do things a certain way, they should really let us know what they want.
>
> **Elaine:** Yes, this is really frustrating.

Adverse Personality Types

We are diverse in our personalities. We are diverse in the way we work, interact, handle conflict, and communicate. Categorizing personality types is often helpful in navigating through diverse characteristics, personalities, work styles, conflict-management styles, and interaction styles in order to allow us to understand the other person better and figure out a better way to interact with them or to interpret their actions. Typically, there are four types of personalities.

Type A Personality:

- Highly independent nature
- Self-driven and aware of the importance of goal setting and motivation
- Competitive
- Highly time conscious
- Often perceived as impatient and could be easily prone to hostility, aggressiveness, and rudeness
- Sharp in getting to the heart of the matter in no-nonsense and blunt terms
- Risk takers
- Highly practical
- Always need to be doing something
- Tend to be workaholics
- Often have a hard time relaxing
- Impatient toward anyone they perceive as incompetent

Type B Personality:

- Essentially the exact opposite of type A personalities
- Hardly stressed, even in seemingly stressful situations
- Extremely relaxed in any situation

- They are usually cheerful and carefree in most situations
- People love hanging out with them
- Entertaining and fun to be around
- Has a lack of urgency
- Although they work hard, they are not stressed about it
- Very patient and maintains the same patience in the most tense and stressful conditions
- Tolerant, flexible, and adaptable
- Complain very rarely
- Very sociable

Type C Personality:

- Introverted
- Detail oriented
- Systematic
- Analytical
- Makes decisions based on research
- Great problem solvers
- Sensitive, deep, and thoughtful
- Logical and likes order
- Reserved
- Conservative and does not like risk
- Critical of others around them
- Does not like being criticized

Type D Personality:

- Likes routine
- Dislikes change
- Good at executing commands
- Hardly feels self-assured
- Tends to experience irritability and worry
- Typically hides negative emotions
- Tends to experience a great deal of stress as a result of negative feelings

It's true that adverse personality types are simply part of human interaction and being, but they are important to keep in mind when managing teams and departments and when trying to engender teamwork. It's important when working toward keeping people engaged, because each of the personality types are motivated by different people and different things. It's also an important factor in creating an ascending company culture, as recognizing the adverse personalities will create sensitivity toward employees' diverse personalities and their diverse needs.

Harmful Communication Patterns

Companies typically suffer from two types of communication issues: they have either got to the point that problems are acute and emotions are heated, which prevents effective communication, or they are lacking or have ineffective communication patterns that lead to conflict.

Effective communication typically cannot happen when emotions are heated, because people are too upset to handle communication effectively. Regardless of whether people are impulsive in their reactions or whether they tend to hold on to anger, effective communication is simply not going to happen.

Effective communication can be defined as those times when messages are heard fully and respectfully on both ends; it's a two-way street. It might seem easy, but communicating effectively actually takes quite a bit of finesse. Choosing the right words, listening with our minds instead of just our ears, and getting our message across are skills that we all need to work on. We will discuss this at length in our chapter "Courageous Conversations," but at this point what is important for us to know is that when conflict is snowballing and people get angry and hurt, effective communication becomes very, very challenging.

> **Typical Scenario:**
>
> **Alan:** Helen, I wanted to talk to you about that meeting with the client yesterday.
>
> **Helen:** Sure, what's up?
>
> **Alan:** How do you think it went?
>
> **Helen:** I think it was fine. Why? Is there a problem?
>
> **Alan:** Well, the client called me and said...well....there may be some issues.
>
> **Helen:** Issues? What happened??
>
> **Alan:** Well, I am not sure. The client said something, I wasn't really sure...let me check with the client again. I'll get back to you.

Even when negative emotions are not at their peak and the snowball has not yet formed (or has not yet fully formed), the following hurdles to effective communication may arise.

Poorly Expressed Messages

When messages are poorly expressed, effective communication is hindered. Because of the obscurity of language, there is always the possibility of misinterpreting messages. This barrier is created because of the wrong choice of words, sequence of sentences, and frequent repetitions. This may be called linguistic chaos. A symbol or a word can have different meanings, and if the receiver misunderstands the communication, it becomes problematic.

Assumptions

We all make assumptions regarding the intentions, motivations, and thought processes of other people. We will talk more about that in our chapter "Assumptions," but it's important to mention here, as assumptions will have an impact on communication. Often, we will hear assumptions in our mind just as loudly as the words that are actually being said. It can be difficult to discern that these are merely our assumptions, though, and sometimes we take them as givens. In that context, the words that are being said are heard and interpreted by us in the context of our own thoughts, and our understanding may be completely different from what the communicator intended.

Body Language
Body language and gestures play a part in all communication, but when that is misunderstood, it hinders the proper understanding of the message. This may especially come into play when we have certain assumptions regarding the intentions (or rather, what we perceive to be the intentions) of the other person, and we may interpret their body language accordingly.

Lack of Attention
When trying to engage in effective communication, attention is paramount. If the receiver is preoccupied with other important work, he/she does not listen to the message attentively. For example, imagine an employee talking to his boss while the latter is busy in some important conversation. In such a situation, the boss may not pay any attention to what the subordinate is saying and misses the point of the message. Thus, there arises psychological hurdles in the communication.

Lack of Trust
For successful communication, the transmitter and the receiver must trust each other. If there is a lack of trust between them, the receiver will often derive an opposite meaning from what was intended. Because of this, communication will become meaningless.

Lack of Proper Incentive

A lack of incentive for the subordinates may create a hindrance in communication. In this instance, a lack of incentive refers to any value or importance given to the employee's suggestion or idea. If the superiors ignore the subordinates, they become indifferent toward any exchange of ideas in future.

> **Dr. Rozen Says:**
> The CLASH model explains the causes for a descending company culture, which are: change, low clarity, adverse personality types, styles of conflict management, and harmful communication patterns.

3

How to Create an Ascending Company Culture, Part I: Creating a Company Culture of FACT

Having to deal with a descending company culture is likely to happen in many companies at one time or another. It may be periodical and then improve, or the need may be consistent. There are some things that you can do and other things that you may want to avoid in order to keep your company culture ascending. In this book, I would like to give you the perfect toolbox for turning a descending company culture into an ascending one, and that's a FACT! So to do that, we will be talking about fostering a culture of FACT, or feedback, adaptability, communication, and teamwork. Successful, growing companies always operate in an environment that reflects the values and skills summarized by the four elements of FACT, and it's these four elements that will improve culture enhancement and turn your company culture from a descending one to an ascending one.

Developing a Company Culture of Feedback
When we talk about developing a company culture of feedback, we have to differentiate between feedback and criticism. The main difference between the two is in the motivation of the speaker. Constructive feedback comes from a place of support, while criticism is fundamentally punitive and so ultimately, the one is positive while the latter is not. People who offer constructive criticism want the best for the people they offer it to; this is considered feedback. That's not the case with non-constructive criticism. It's not as simple as just expecting feedback to happen, though. If an organizational environment is going to be one in which people give and receive feedback freely, the top management must make it clear that they want it. More importantly, they must be prepared to model it themselves—particularly, how to receive it—thus setting a good example for employees to follow. Employers should provide employees with explicit expectations and guidelines for giving and receiving constructive criticism.

So what makes constructive feedback effective? One of the most important considerations when giving feedback is to make the experience as positive as possible. That doesn't mean always giving glowing reviews, of course—although it would be nice if that could happen! Instead, it's about creating a positive environment, especially as constructive feedback often has a negative feeling around it. Many of us shudder involuntarily, for example, at the mere mention of the words "performance evaluation." While a performance evaluation clearly is a type of feedback and is usually intended to be constructive, these sorts of evaluations often don't take place as frequently as they could. As a result, annual and semiannual performance evaluations can become emotionally devastating, as six or twelve months' worth of shortcomings are dumped on our heads all at once. In order to avoid overwhelming employees with a comprehensive list of their failings, it's important to provide informal feedback consistently and frequently, on a weekly or even daily basis, so that the catalogue of issues that must eventually be discussed during formal performance evaluations is neither unexpected nor overwhelming. The other benefit, of course, is that by providing feedback more frequently, the employee becomes emotionally habituated to it.

There are additional factors, too. Feedback that is provided as soon as possible after the incident that provoked it, for example, gives employees the best chance of understanding their error in their own terms, and they find it easier to make the appropriate corrections. Giving feedback this way, moreover, means that it's spread out over time. No more than two, or at the most, three, issues should be discussed at once; a longer list is likely to be disheartening and therefore counterproductive. It's also important to remember to focus on positives whenever possible. Not only does providing praise when praise is due bolster employees' self-confidence, it shows them what success looks like and hopefully drives them to want more of it! Bearing this in mind, though: it is important to remember to praise in public but to ensure that constructive criticism is offered discreetly. Having their failings aired in front of their colleagues is unlikely to engender positive feelings from an employee, and this will ultimately affect their work. Above all, it's critical to remember that a harsh or punitive experience really doesn't teach an employee anything except to loathe the experience and to do anything to avoid it in the future.

In addition to being delivered in a positive way, effective constructive criticism has four major characteristics, which I have abbreviated to the WWWH Questions: when, what, why, and how. The "when" issue addresses the timing of the incident that provoked the feedback. Knowing precisely when a behavioral lapse occurred makes the memory of it sharper in the employee's mind. Clearly, the better employees understand exactly what they did wrong, the more likely they will be able to correct it.

The "what" issue also helps employees understand specifically what they need to work on. When you tell an employee what she did improperly, be sure to limit your comments to what you know firsthand. Bringing up issues you know of through word of mouth can cause resentment between employees and damage morale. Moreover, you can never be sure of the accuracy of these secondhand reports.

When broaching issues with employees, it's a good idea to prepare your general comments in advance, because you are more likely to remain objective and stick to the issues at hand. When you describe problematic behavior, do so by using "I" statements, because they will help you avoid labeling the employee. Say, "I was disappointed and concerned that you didn't bother to check the accuracy of your references yesterday" instead of, "You were irresponsible yesterday." Most importantly, tell the person exactly what he needs to improve on, and stick to the facts to prevent ambiguity. If you tell someone she acted unprofessionally for example, what exactly does that mean? Were they too loud, too unfriendly, too coarse, too flip, or too poorly dressed?

The "why" of the issue is also important. Although the "why" may seem self-evident to you, it might be a complete mystery to your employee. Never assume an employee understands the full implications of a professional mistake but instead discuss why it's important to behave differently. Indeed, new employees may resent being called to task for doing something if they don't understand the risk they ran or the damage they did.

Perhaps the most important characteristic of effective feedback is the "how" issue—providing explicit instructions on how performance should be improved in a specific area. The best kind of objective to give an employee is one that has specific and measurable characteristics, with a well-defined timeline and a well defined and measurable goal. Ideally, objectives should also be at least partly set by the employee, because then he or she is much more likely to take ownership of them. Finally, you should be sure to follow up on any objectives that you and your employee have agreed to. Slacking off on the follow-up snatches defeat from the jaws of victory by sending the message to the employee that your concern was not serious.

What Creates a Culture of Feedback within Companies?

Feedback should happen throughout the year and should be provided by everyone, regardless of their position in the company, as feedback provides valuable information to the receiver. You don't have to agree with it, but it is important to hear it. Giving and receiving feedback will be discussed in detail in my chapter on Courageous Conversations, but for now, it's important to remember that the ultimate source of a culture of constructive feedback must be top management. Senior managers must solicit it for themselves and consider it when offered. They must offer it to their subordinates and colleagues as one team member to another, in a transparent effort to improve the chances of collective success.

> **Typical Scenario:**
>
> **Shelly:** I just had my weekly meeting with Ron.
>
> **Charlie:** And? How did it go?
>
> **Shelly:** All he does is criticize me.
>
> **Charlie:** Really? Why?
>
> **Shelly:** It is literally half an hour of everything that I did wrong. By the time I get out of there, my work day is over. I simply cannot do anything and I feel like going home.

Promoting a Company Culture of Adaptability
The way we live today changes rapidly, and this most definitely includes the way we work with clients in the course of our everyday professional lives. You need to ask yourself two questions in this context: first, can your team or company adapt to the changes it faces? And second, can your team adjust to new technologies and innovations? Adaptability is considered to be the single most important factor for human survival in general, and it is just as important for the survival of your company.

To do well as a leader within your company and to build an adaptable team, you need to be able to accomplish five things. First, you need to create a corporate culture that recognizes the opportunity in every challenge. Second, you need to recognize and focus on the right priorities. Third, you must be committed to clear and productive communication, both within the company and with customers and clients. Fourth, you must ensure that responsibilities are clearly defined and that each employee is unambiguously accountable for specific organizational functions. Finally, you must promote and nurture creativity and entrepreneurship at all levels of the organization.

Embrace Change—There Is an Opportunity within It
There are many stories about companies that were once leaders in their field that have fallen behind, because of their inability to recognize their need to change and to implement the necessary measures. We can't stop change, and we should not be surprised when it happens. Change is inevitable. The vital

question regarding change is how it comes to us and how flexibly and rapidly we can adapt to it. Moreover, we should never forget that those dreaded changes in the market shouldn't always be so dreaded. They are not only a threat but they are also an opportunity for growth—if only we, as corporate leaders, can recognize it. There is a simple difference between a successful company and a failing one, and it is this: rather than resisting external pressure to change, successful companies are striving constantly to position themselves ahead of a change *before* it happens. Bare corporate survival demands, at a minimum, that we can react rapidly and efficiently to major changes in our business sector.

Fostering a Company Culture of Communication

Do people in your company feel heard? Are leaders within the company open to new ideas? Is it acceptable for everyone within the company to come up with ideas, no matter what their position is? Is management transparent, open, and honest with all employees? Workplace communication is the transmission of information from one person or group to another person or group in an organization. It can include face-to-face communication, e-mails, text messages, voicemails, notes, and so on.

Important Advantages
Workplace communication is vital to an organization's ability to be productive and to operate smoothly. There are at least three major benefits to effective workplace communication. They are as follows:

1. Workplace communication improves worker productivity. Research shows that effective lateral and work group communication leads to an improvement in overall company performance. It has also been discovered that employees who were graded highest in productivity had received the most effective communication from their superiors. Consider the following example.

   Gertrude works in engineering for a toy manufacturer, and her prototypes of toys receive accolades. She is effective in communicating the advantages of her designs and how children will play with them in real life. In return, she receives specific guidance from her superiors, allowing her to create designs quickly and efficiently.

   In this instance, effective communication has led to increased productivity.

2. Workplace communication can increase employee job satisfaction. Employees feel empowered if they are able to communicate with senior management. This type of communication happens when information flows upward in an organization, and it usually consists of employees providing feedback to their superiors. If bosses or managers are able to listen to employees and respond appropriately, this two-way communication usually leads to an increase in employee job satisfaction.

   Employees are also happy when there is intense downward communication, when there is information flowing down from superiors or managers. In our previous toy factory example, Gertrude recently sent an e-mail to her boss recommending that her department upgrade its design software. Her upward communication feedback was not just acknowledged—it was acted on, resulting in both a very happy design team and a happy Gertrude, as she felt valued and heard.
3. Workplace communication can also have a positive effect on absenteeism and turnover rates. Communication flow is very important to workers. Employees have to feel confident that they are receiving truthful and updated information from superiors. They also want to have the ability to share ideas, thoughts, and concerns within the company. Studies have shown that even after a layoff, companies with excellent communication are able to retain the surviving employees.

Whether your team is distributed across several offices or is located under one roof, here are four ways that you can create an environment centered on the open, two-way communication that builds cohesion.

1. Transparency
A common mistake that management teams make is not sharing information throughout the organization. This demonstrates a lack of confidence, and, as a result, it can lead to distrust. The best way to prevent this is to practice open, transparent communication. It's a good idea to share information throughout your organization, as it creates an environment of trust and a feeling of being in it together. Concerns about overwhelming your teams are almost always unfounded. The people you want to hire in a startup are those who are smart and ambitious enough to want this information and those who will use it to make the company better.

2. Inter-departmental collaboration
Many workplace failures stem from lack of collaboration and poor communication. This secretive, single unit approach divides people and can lead to interdepartmental friction. When employees aren't communicating across departments, leaders should identify this as soon as possible, and immediately put into place practices that strengthen relationships between different teams. At my company, we have a strong culture of open feedback and communication, but this is something

we've built over time by establishing genuine human connections. For instance, we bring together our globally distributed team for a daily video call to celebrate recent successes and to gather support for challenges.

Bringing people together in this way really does work. Always look for ways to build connections between people, especially when there's a lack of common work goals and interests. Open office layouts, group lunches, team outings, and retreats can encourage collaboration and sharing.

3. Clarity regarding roles and rules

Often, a lack of alignment within a team directly diminishes productivity. If employees don't know what their roles are or what the rules are, their productivity levels are bound to suffer. On the  other hand, employees who have clear roles, responsibilities, and deadlines are more likely to be held accountable—and they're more likely to hold themselves accountable. In any situation where rules and roles are not completely clear, make sure everything is spelled out. Vagueness is conflict's biggest ally.

4. Diversity awareness in all communications

Cross-cultural communication is imperative for companies that have a diverse workforce and participate in the global economy, so it's important for employees to understand the factors that play a part in an effective, diverse workforce. Cross-cultural communication has become strategically important to companies due to the growth of global business, technology, and the Internet. As a result, understanding cross-cultural communication is important for any company with a diverse workforce or a business plan that entails global operations. This type of communication involves an understanding of how people from different cultures speak or communicate and how they perceive the world around them.

Cross-cultural communication in an organization, then, deals with understanding different business customs, beliefs, and communication strategies. Language differences, high-context versus low-context cultures, nonverbal variances, and power distances are all major factors that can affect cross-cultural communication.

The biggest problem in dealing with cross-cultural communication, of course, is the difficulty created by language barriers. In addition to explicitly linguistic barriers (i.e., speaking different languages), gestures and patterns of eye contact are two areas of nonverbal communication that are utilized differently across cultures. Companies must train employees in the correct way to handle

nonverbal communication in such a way as to avoid offending people from other cultures. For example, American workers tend to wave their hands and use a finger to point when giving nonverbal directions. Extreme gesturing is considered rude in some cultures. While pointing may be considered appropriate in many contexts in the United States, Yamato would never use a finger to point toward another person, because that gesture is considered rude in Japan. He might instead gesture with an open hand, with his palm facing up, toward the person being addressed.

Encouraging a Company Culture of Teamwork

Fostering teamwork means creating a work culture that encourages collaboration. In a strong teamwork environment, people understand and believe that thinking, planning, decisions, and actions are done best when done cooperatively. People recognize and eventually come to believe in the notion that "none of us is as good as all of us." So teams work together to accomplish a common goal.

Teams are a part of business, so there is no hiding from the importance of teamwork. Teams make things, accomplish tasks, provide services, offer advice, and seek to meet other goals. While people have used teams to come together and accomplish tasks since we were hunters and gatherers, the concept is always evolving. And today, more and more companies are incorporating teams of a variety of sizes and types into their workflows.

Here are the four major types of teams:

Departmental Teams
Departmental teams perform specific functions in an organization. Members of these teams are from the same department or work area, and they meet regularly.

Interdisciplinary Teams
Workers from across different functions or specialties within the organization make up these types of teams. People with separate areas of expertise work together; they are usually at about the same hierarchical level and can often make decisions without management. Often, these teams are temporary.

Leadership Teams
Management takes a strategic role in guiding business decisions, so leadership teams are made up of leaders from varied departments. The goals of leadership teams are generally aligned with the overall mission and vision of the company.

Project Teams
Project teams consist of individuals who are often from different disciplines or department but who are brought together for the purpose of a specific task or an important project.

Benefits of Teamwork
When people work together toward a common goal in an atmosphere of trust and accountability, they put aside any turf

issues and politics and instead focus on the tasks to be done. This focus of resources overcomes barriers, helps to identify new opportunities, and builds a momentum that leads to three major bottom-line benefits:

1. Better problem solving
2. Greater productivity
3. More effective use of resources

These benefits happen because

1. people enjoy working together, and teamwork satisfies a need for socialization;
2. working together helps people grow as they learn from each other and develop important skills; and
3. working together toward a common goal provides a sense of purpose that is motivating and fulfilling.

Need I say more about the benefits of teamwork?

Team Characteristics
Productive teams usually share many characteristics. They have a common purpose that each member is committed to. They stay involved until the objective is completed. They care about each other, and in keeping with

this, they are concerned about how their actions and attitudes affect one another. They listen to each other, respect all points of view, and are sensitive to each other's needs. Their leaders engender this atmosphere by encouraging everyone's participation in the decision-making process.

If you look at groups of employees who work well as teams, you would see these characteristics or traits:

Openness
The more reluctant people are to express their feelings and be honest with each other, the more likely suspicion and distrust will exist. When real teamwork is present, team members, are more open and honest with each other because they basically trust each other.

Acceptance of assignments.
It would be nice if we could choose all our own work, but that's unrealistic! Sometimes, we've got to do the jobs that we don't necessarily like, and this is true with teamwork, too. Still, when real teamwork exists, team members willingly accept assignments. Motivated by peer pressure, they also work hard to get their jobs done right the first time and to meet deadlines.

Understood and accepted goals.
A team needs purpose, direction, and goals. In strong teams, these goals are both understood and accepted by each of the members, and they work collaboratively to achieve them. Their

manager will have explained the importance of achieving these goals in the bigger corporate picture, and as a result, team members fully understand why they are being asked to reach these goals. Committed to their accom-  plishment, they assist one another to make their goals a reality. So in this instance, acceptance and understanding really do help productivity.

Progress and results assessed.
Teamwork requires that members be results directed as opposed to process oriented. Their focus is on their objectives, and their activities are directed toward those goals. In other words, they focus on the end instead of their means of getting there. Periodically, under direction from a leader, the team assesses its progress, and that knowledge serves to guide future team action. This includes identification of barriers and what can be done to get rid of them.

Shared trust.
In a healthy team, members essentially trust one another. Although there may be an occasional conflict, members get along well and enjoy each other's company. They cooperate and get the work done.

Involvement and participation.
There are three general types of people in the world: those who do not know or care about what is happening, those who watch what others do, and those who make things happen. Teamwork requires that members be involved in their work and participate in team activities, so the most productive team members are those who make things happen. What they say and do counts for something. When teamwork works best, members are involved in decision making and practice participative management.

The Two Most Common Problems When It Comes to Teamwork:
Teamwork simply does not exist.
Many departments don't operate as teams or practice teamwork. Members may talk to each other at the printer or over lunch, and their work efforts may be designed to meet the overarching objectives of the department, but these employees' work on a day-to-day basis is largely done as individuals. This is unfortunate, for many business experts now believe that teamwork is critical to organizational productivity and profitability.

Loners within Teams.
"Loners" typically have a territorial, introverted, or us-versus-them or even me-versus-you attitude. They tend to be workers who simply don't want to be team players. This type of worker

may produce work of value in her own right but can also create much resentment from other team members or spark conflict with colleagues. Loners cannot be changed. It's simply their personality to work alone, and the whole teamwork concept is foreign and uncomfortable to them. If they are truly valuable to the company, and often they are, you will have to work closely with them in order to prevent negative situations. The Red-Shift Blue-Shift model goes a long way in helping lone workers and the conflicts they may have, because those lone workers often operate based on their sense of being threatened by others within the team. The Red-Shift Blue-Shift model disarms this.

> **Dr. Rozen Says:**
> Create a company culture of FACT by enhancing: feedback, adaptability, communication, and teamwork.

4

How to Create an Ascending Company Culture. Part II: Soaring to New Heights with the Red-Shift Blue-Shift Model

"Red shift" and "Blue shift" are two concepts that come from the world of astronomy, but I believe they can be applied to business as well, and the analogy between the world of human interaction and the interaction of stars and galaxies has always fascinated me. Together, the red and blue shifts create the Doppler effect. In space, when an object or a galaxy moves away from you, it appears red on the spectrum of colors. When an object or a galaxy moves toward you in space, it appears blue. As the different galaxies move around in space, they may impact each other, but they wouldn't be fully visible to each other. They would only see the aspects of the other galaxy that are exposed to them. To relate this back to humans, I always like to think that people, like galaxies, are an entire world of experiences, personality traits, interpretation of experiences, and unique characteristics. What's more, not all aspects of the other people that surround them are visible to them: what they are going through, what motivates them, what their intentions are, and so on. Like galaxies in space, we shift closer and further away from other people and so create our own red and blue shifts.

Descending company cultures are characterized by a high level of red-shift dynamics: people shift away from each other and away from teamwork, trust, and collaboration. Ascending company cultures have a much higher level of blue-shift dynamics: people demonstrate a high level of teamwork, feel engaged and motivated, have good problem-solving skills, and work well together toward productivity and success. Unfortunately, there are many occasions when our instinctual behavior would draw us toward red-shift actions, especially in challenging situations. The goal of the Red-Shift Blue-Shift model is to control instinctual behavior that may lead to a red-shift effect and to train employees toward blue-shift-oriented behavior that is so typical of ascending company cultures. Ultimately, this blue-shift behavior demonstrates adaptability, a high level of engagement, productivity, growth, and success—so turning everyone blue would be ideal!

Red-Shift Actions and Their Impact on Company Culture

The human psyche is a complicated one. By no means can we compare workplace dynamics to dynamics in the jungle.

Or can we?

You see, conflicts, and especially acute conflicts, take us right back to where we started as a species: to animalistic behavior. Now we may wear professional clothing; we may drive cars, fly business class, and have cell phones. And hopefully we do not show up to work dangling from trees or beating our chests. But in fact, in our own way, and with a human twist, we manifest animal like characteristics in our instincts when we encounter conflict. This is typically reflected in what I call the URGE factor:

Unleash attack
Recruit pack
Guard territory
Exercise self-defense

When we let our animalistic instincts impact our choices of conduct and behavior in the workplace, this results in a descending company culture and in red-shift dynamics. Employees, teams, and departments drift away from each other; collaboration and productivity are reduced, and as a result, so is the company's overall success. It starts from small undercurrents and shifts to bigger and more harmful dynamics. The URGE factor basically describes how we let our instinctual reactions direct our choices and our dynamics with fellow employees.

Unleash Attack
The most likely reason for attacking someone personally would have to do with feeling threatened. When we feel threatened

by another person—in terms of our position, prestige, image, or opportunities—we unleash an attack. This would usually manifest itself in negative behavior in the form of aggressive or passive-aggressive words, e-mails, body language, or strategies that would target the "other" whom we perceive as dangerous to our survival in the workplace. Passive-aggressive behaviors can manifest themselves as things like deliberately missing deadlines, deliberate incompletion of assignments, non-sharing of information, and more. Verbal aggression can refer to demeaning and intimidating others by belittling them, embarrassing them, and more.

The impact of unleashing an attack in the workplace, in any possible format, is devastating. After all, our ultimate goal is to create, foster, and highlight teamwork. When an attack occurs, or a series of them occurs on an ongoing basis, there is no team; instead there are opposing sides. Once that happens, it is hard to create teamwork, as colleagues have become opponents—they're no longer on the same side or team. They may believe they have suffered an attack from another employee, and they may still be licking their wounds. What's interesting is that while in some cases we can clearly see what the trigger for unleashing the attack has been, in other cases the trigger is unclear. In the latter case, the subject of the attack and perhaps even the surrounding workplace environment are unable to see what the trigger was, and even if they do identify it, they don't see the connection between that possible trigger and the intensity of the unleashed attack. In other words, they often feel that their colleague has overreacted.

One of the reasons that this disparity may occur is that the trigger is not simply a trigger but instead is always linked with an interpretation and meaning that the person assigns to it; his or her own personal history; where he or she is in his or her life at this point; other things he or she may be going through; and his or her own sensitivities, fears, and concerns. So the trigger is actually built upon much more than one simple action, but when that trigger causes someone to unleash an attack, that attack creates an immediate red-shift impact. Just as objects and galaxies separate in astrology, so this red shift among teams denotes people who draw away from each other, damaging teamwork and increasing everyone's anxiety and hostility.

Recruit Pack
People who are in conflict with someone look to other people in their social and workplace environment to justify and agree with their perception of the rival as negative, and so they typically recruit a "pack"—much like wolves do! By doing this, they connect with other people, persuading them to agree on their negative views of the rival.

Recruiting a pack is beneficial, because it validates their interpretation of the other's action as aggressive, even if this isn't objectively true. Recruiting a pack, then, makes people feel empowered and prevents them from having to evaluate their own actions, behavior, and interpretation of the situation. Every interpersonal interaction is subjective and can be interpreted in different ways by different people, but recruiting a pack causes people to believe that their subjective interpretation is in fact the ultimate truth, simply because there is a pack of other people at the office who agree with them. In other words, if other members of the group think that their behavior is acceptable, then they feel that there is no reason to doubt themselves.

Recruiting a pack is closely linked to our confirmation bias: the unconscious act of teaming up with those people who would validate or fuel our own views while at the same time ignoring or dismissing any other opinions that threaten our perception or interpretation of certain interpersonal dynamics. Because we team up with people who agree with us and prefer to distance ourselves from those who do not, we basically create our own validation group. We think to ourselves, "I can't be wrong, because all those people say the same thing." The reality may very well be that there are many more people who think very differently; we just do not want to count them in, and as a result, we quickly dismiss their views.

Typical Scenario:

Carol: That Jamie is really out of control. This is such a problem. Everyone hates working with him.

Alison: Really? Usually he and I get along just fine.

Carol: Oh, yes. Definitely. I talked to Sharon from accounting and to Darren from Sales and they both agreed with me. Everyone keeps telling me 'Jamie did this' and 'Jamie did that'. Honestly, that's all I hear these days.

Alison: Really? I had no clue.

Guard Territory
People are territorial by nature. We are territorial on an international level, but we are also territorial on a smaller scale at work. When we feel threatened by a fellow coworker, a new policy, or organizational change, we typically go into a "guard territory" phase. This instinctual behavior is an interesting one in the context of workplace dynamics, because it's something that is both positive and negative. After all, we want employees to have ownership of their work, because it increases engagement. The problem is, though, there is a fine line between ownership and guarding territory. In descending company cultures, where trust is low and the atmosphere is conflict saturated, not only do employees tend to guard their territory more often and more fiercely, but this behavior is also typically not judged as non-team-oriented by their fellow employees. To some extent, that behavior may become part of the company's culture and norm.

Exercise Self-Defense
Our self-defense instinct goes immediately into action when we feel threatened or attacked. This instinct means that we would do anything and everything in order to protect ourselves, and any choice we make in terms of our conduct and interactions is justified, because survival (and in this case, workplace survival) is paramount. Self-defense when we feel attacked may include some or all of the following:

- Aggressive behavior toward the perceived danger
- Passive-aggressive behavior toward the perceived danger
- Attempts to manipulate the environment in order to eliminate the threat
- Excessive focus on rules and regulations as a means of seeking protection
- Becoming overly critical, bossy, and controlling of others
- Competitive and sectarian behavior

> **Typical Scenario:**
>
> **Matt:** I feel that Jake is out to get me. He keeps taking weird notes in his office. I feel that he is documenting things.
>
> **Sarah:** Seriously? Why would he?
>
> **Matt:** Me and him, we never got along. I am telling you, he is after me.
>
> **Sarah:** That's horrible.
>
> **Matt:** Don't worry. I am after him already. He is up for a few surprises that I have planned for him.

> **Dr. Rozen Says:**
> The URGE Factor stands for instinctual behaviors that may cause conflict saturated company cultures. URGE stands for unleash attack, recruit pack, guard territory, and exercise self-defense. The URGE factor leads to a red shift effect, which means that departments, team members, and people in general shift away from each other.

Categorizing Red-Shift Dynamics

There are four main categories to red-shift dynamics. These are tunnel vision, avoidance, assuming, and the one-solution approach. It's critical to pay attention to these, as they provide insight into where we may fail as teams and what we should do to overcome **those hurdles.**

Tunnel Vision

Tunnel vision is exactly as it sounds: narrow, single-tracked vision. It can happen in any circumstance whereby our perception is narrowed to that situation only, blocking out the bigger picture. What does this mean? It means that we interpret and assign meaning to the situation in a very constricted manner. Let's look at the following case study as an example.

> *There is an office conflict over not handing in a report on time. Mary doesn't accept my position and wants me to fail, but she is lazy and incompetent, has never liked me from the get-go, and is hard to get along with. She does not care about the team.*

This is an example of tunnel vision, because the person complaining about Mary is not thinking about anything other than his or her own narrow perceptions. Of course, it may be that Mary genuinely is lazy and incompetent! In reality though, it is more likely that Mary has personal problems or health problems, she might be going through troubles, or she might have been unclear about the expectations. In fact, it could be all of the above.

What fuels tunnel vision is our human tendency to do two things: to focus primarily on ourselves and to assign meaning to events by inventing narratives. In terms of the former, we generally consider ourselves to be social and considerate, but often we are not. Instead, we see the world through our own lenses, and these lenses make us focus primarily on ourselves. We are designed around the need to feel good about ourselves. We want to think that we're wonderful—although we all know that sometimes we aren't! If we can't be wonderful then at least we would like to think that we are pretty close.

Here are three major ways that we overestimate ourselves:

1. We think we're nicer than we actually are.

In a study at Cornell, participants were asked if they would donate to charity. A staggering 80 percent said that they would, but the results of the study suggest otherwise. The researchers found that over the course of two experiments, only half of those who said they would donate actually did when given the chance. And it gets worse, because those who did donate gave only half as much as they previously said they would.

What's strange is that while they were wrong about what they would donate, the amount of money donated in reality was close to what the participants predicted others would contribute. So they overestimated how much they would give but got it right when predicting how much others would give. You could say that we have a pretty accurate idea of how selfish the rest of the world is, but in our imaginations, we don't perceive ourselves as being members of that world. Perhaps instead we all picture ourselves as members of an elite moral minority.

It wasn't just with money, either. Another study involved predicting whether participants would take on a complex task rather than an easy one when they knew somebody else would get stuck with the task they didn't take. Most people thought, "Of course I'll do the harder task! It's only fair," but when actually presented with the task, they were far more likely to pawn it off on the other person—even when they were told that person was a ten-year-old girl!

2. We think that our problems are the worst.

Studies have found that we perceive our pain, our unhappiness, and the things that bother us, as much, much worse than anything that others go through. We also assume that our lives are worse and that we are unhappier than those around us.

Part of this self-pity is due to the fact that it's a social norm for everyone to project only the good things about their lives—we like to brag about the positives while burying the negatives! As the author of the study pointed out, just look at people's Facebook photo albums—it's all parties, vacations, the new puppy, the new girlfriend, the new TV, and the gang laughing at a bar. Nobody posts photos of themselves straining on the toilet and screaming that their colon is full of burning rocks. And your photos are probably just as carefree as theirs. This also makes sense when you compare it with the study about generosity from earlier, where people basically paint themselves as heroes. If our suffering is worse than other people's, then damn it, we're downright heroic just for enduring it.

3. We like to think of ourselves in more heroic terms than we actually deserve.

We all have a narrative in our head regarding who we are and how we operate, and because we always prefer to think of ourselves in favorable terms, that narrative often portrays us as heroic. For example, in a situation where we are in conflict with another person, we naturally think of ourselves as the one who was right, imagining that we were suffering from the other person's bad actions, and yet we still managed to overcome the obstacle. Our internal narrative might tell us that we were handling the situation heroically, even though we may in fact be at fault. This narrative is clearly only in our heads, and it is quite funny to think that the other person, who may also be experiencing much suffering, will be thinking of themselves in similarly heroic terms. The truth is, probably neither of them is heroic! We prefer this heroic narrative, because it feeds into our favorite narrative of ourselves as good, positive, just, and right. Thinking of ourselves as heroes in terms of how we deal with the situation is now just the cherry on the ice cream.

So how does this link up with the resolution of workplace conflict? To understand that, we have to look at the close link between conflict and narrative identity.

Narrative identity, then, is the story that we tell ourselves about our lives, and we do this to create meaning. Our story is almost always positive, as that is how we like to see ourselves. Because we all have these narrative identities, there is no such thing as "the ultimate truth" about any situation. I have heard people say things like: "There is my story, his story, and the real story." My point is, I guess, that there is no real story. Reality is in the eye of the beholder, and it will always and forever be impacted by the meaning that we ascribe to it. People ascribe different meanings to different situations, and this happens in the workplace, too.

In a given workplace conflict, each person interprets the situation differently based on their own narrative identity. They interpret it in a way that would feed their narrative of themselves as heroes, as just and right, as wonderful people, and as victims of the situation. If they interpret it in any other way, it would mean that their narrative about themselves as good, hardworking, and positive people would be cracked and damaged—and no one wants to think that about themselves! So where there is fault, person A will blame person B, regardless of where the fault actually lies. "It's not my fault," they say, and even if they were willing to admit that they had some level of responsibility in the conflict, they would keep it to a minimum, because they would rather believe their own narrative that they are wonderful people who were just unlucky enough to find themselves involved with that other, difficult person.

In one of my all-time favorite episodes of the BBC sitcom *Fawlty Towers*, Basil Fawlty goes to apologize to one of the hotel guests about some miserable incident. He rehearses his apology to himself as he travels to the guest's hotel room—"I'm so sorry; I made a mistake"—over and over again, but as soon as the poor guest opens his door, Basil turns to him and says almost instantly, "I'm so sorry…my wife has made a mistake!" Basil just couldn't bring himself to admit that he had messed up. After all, this works against his narrative of himself as a wonderful, service-oriented hotel owner. How much easier it is to put the blame on the other, whoever that other may be: the wife, circumstances—anything but the self.

To take this back, then, tunnel vision feeds into that perception exactly. We look at a conflict or an undesirable or unpleasant clash with another person in a very narrow way. We focus primarily on the interaction that we currently have with that person, not taking into account any other possible stressors or impacting factors on that person's behavior. We are not taking into consideration their personal life, their culture, possible misunderstandings, and so on. As a result, we assign meaning to our interaction from what we see with our tunnel vision.

I always like to think of people as diamonds. Just as the stones are multifaceted, so are people. We are multidimensional in our interactions with others, and sometimes, only one side of the diamond is exposed or visible in the same way that sometimes only one dimension of our lives is visible. Our spouses and friends are not always fully exposed to how we behave at work, for example. Our kids likewise see a completely different and often one-dimensional side of us; our parents see yet another. Together, all these different dimensions of our lives create the full diamond of who we are.

Tunnel vision has four main patterns that interrupt the goal of teamwork and deepen conflicts.

1. We judge ourselves more favorably than we judge others. Judging ourselves more favorably than we judge others really just feeds into our personal narrative of being

overall wonderful people. Judging ourselves more favorably is very likely to happen, because when it comes to our own actions, we have a lot of background information that helps us explain why we did what we did or behaved how we behaved. We know that we had a bad day that day, that we didn't feel well. We can compare the situation to other situations and say that this behavior is atypical of us, and so on. We will look at the situation through very self-forgiving lenses. When it comes to the other person involved, however, things are a bit different. First of all, we don't have sufficient information about her to put her behavior into context, and even if we think that we do, it's insignificant compared to the amount of information that we have about ourselves.

It's not just that, either. We constantly operate under our subconscious wish to glorify ourselves in order to feed into the narrative that we are wonderful, good people and wonderful employees. For that reason, in our subjective interpretation of the other's behavior, we would be more likely to assume that she is not as wonderful as we are, that her motives are not as pure, and that this is where her behavior stems from. Tunnel vision feeds exactly into that, because we judge the other person in a very narrow manner, just on the basis of our particular situation, whereas we judge our own behavior from a much wider perspective.

2. **We attribute our behaviors to external circumstances and others' behaviors to internal character traits.**
In social psychology, this is called the fundamental attribution error. This means that when it comes to explaining the behavior of the people around us, we tend to put the emphasis on internal factors ("He did this because he wanted to hurt me, or because he was looking for revenge," for example) rather than on possible external factors ("He did it because he was having a hard day, or because he has a lot on his plate"). This tendency to believe that people behave a certain way because they are out to get us or don't respect us is very problematic. We dismiss the possibility of this being subjective interpretation, and instead, we absolutely believe our own viewpoint. It's not correct, though. We are so unaware of so many possible external reasons for that behavior, and often we are so engulfed in our own interpretation that we don't even consider external factors as an option. We think: she didn't call me because she doesn't care enough to call. Perhaps she doesn't care, but the chances are that she didn't call us because she is sick or forgot or just had a fight with her spouse—we just haven't thought of those options.

When we decide that the other person behaved in a certain way because of those intrinsic unfavorable feelings they have toward us, we build an entire theory about it; we distance ourselves from the person; and we seek validation from others around us. So does this lead to teamwork? No, not really.

3. We tend to favor negative impressions.

Our tendency to focus more on negative impressions is called the negativity bias. The bias basically highlights our tendency to focus on things that are negative and unpleasant more than on things that are happy and pleasant. Even if we are optimistic, happy people, these types of events and feelings have greater influence over us and over our actions. This means that traumas, unpleasant interactions, and unpleasant feelings will have more impact on our behavioral choices than positive ones.

In the context of interpersonal behavior, it is a bias that we should work to overcome. It may cause us to judge the people around us based on the negative aspect of our interaction with them rather than based on good things that might have happened. In other words, we are picking out the bad and ignoring the good—and that certainly won't help us when it comes to interpersonal relationships!

4. We assume that others are similar to us and then judge them for being different.

This interesting dynamic is called the false consensus bias. This is where we tend to assume that other people's values, beliefs, and preferences are similar to ours. Furthermore, we believe that our own beliefs, values, and preferences are normal, right, and just. Then upon discovering that others don't share our ideal values, we find ourselves disappointed with them and judge them for it. The false consensus effect certainly feeds into our positive narrative about ourselves ("Here are the desired values, and here we are, matching them perfectly!"), and this boosts our positive view of ourselves. Our problem is that this stands in the way of our interaction with others. The false consensus bias manifests itself in tunnel vision dynamics, because we judge the other person's beliefs and behaviors through the very narrow lens of our own beliefs, which we consider to be not only the norm but also desirable. This causes a significant red-shift effect:

1. *I expect you to have the same values as me and to behave accordingly. This is because I know what is "right."*
2. *You did not behave as I had expected, based on my values, which I assumed we both shared.*
3. *How could you do that? You must have done that on purpose, or perhaps you just don't care!*
4. *I will get you for that, believe me, the next chance I get.*
5. *You are definitely not on my team, buddy. You and I have an issue.*

And so on.

In this dynamic, it doesn't even occur to us that our values are not the ultimate values, that the other person is entitled to her own values, or that the fact that she didn't meet our expectations doesn't mean necessarily that she is out to get us, does not respect us, or does not care.

Taking this all back to the workplace, tunnel vision causes us to red shift from the other person or group in a conflict-saturated company culture. This means that it draws us away from the other person when we have a conflict with them. When we perceive people from a tunnel vision perspective, we don't take the time or make the effort to keep in mind where they are coming from or what they might be going through, and as a result, our tunnel vision keeps us away from them and deepens possible anger. This is especially bad considering that they are very likely to be looking at us from a tunnel vision perspective as well!

Here are the five steps to red shifting from someone as a result of tunnel vision:

>   Step 1: We do not fully understand the situation, because we are looking at it in a one-dimensional and narrow manner (tunnel vision).
>   Step 2: We assign the situation a meaning that basically exists only in our own head.
>   Step 3: We get mad at the other due to our own assigned meaning, which may have nothing to do with what is actually happening.

Step 4: Our own invented narrative that resulted from our tunnel vision causes us anger and resentment toward the other.

Step 5: We shift away from the other: red shift.

Flipping this around, using peripheral vision in our dealings with other people means that we take into consideration a variety of factors that may come into play as a cause for the other person's behavior. It is the opposite of tunnel vision and leads to a blue-shift effect, meaning that it brings people closer to each other. It's important to remember that having a frustrating situation with a coworker does not necessarily mean that he or she is doing anything to spite or disrespect us. Here is what the peripheral vision offers as possible reasons for actions that may cause anger and frustration:

Diversity of culture and values.

The workplace consists of individuals who all have their own perspectives of the world. Some employees have strong beliefs that they are unwilling to compromise. These beliefs can clash with coworkers' beliefs, creating conflict. For example, if one individual strongly opposes workplace diversity, he may have trouble accepting other workers different from him. To avoid conflict with these workers, he must try to accept or initiate more tolerance of those with differing values.

Diversity of personalities.
No two people are exactly alike. Therefore, personality clashes in the workplace are unavoidable. One employee may have a reserved personality while another may be more outgoing and forward. Problems arise when the two don't understand or respect each other's inner nature.

Managers have the difficult task of overseeing diverse teams in the workplace and finding ways for them to be as productive, creative, and efficient as possible. While this may seem like an impossible task, it's not impossible to create harmony in a diverse environment. The key is understanding these different office personality types and how to motivate them and keep them happily working together.

Each of us has our own natural style of thinking, processing information, problem solving, and communicating. Conflict often arises when communication appears to be at a standstill or when someone has miscommunicated his or her message. By learning to give the other person the information he or she needs, in the manner that he or she can process it most efficiently, you can actually increase productivity and create a more harmonious work environment.

Take a look at the different personality types below. Identify your colleagues and direct reports, and use their personality strengths to drive results in your organization.

The Group Leaders focus on tasks, goals, and the bottom line. They take charge and make decisions quickly even if they don't have all the details. Often, they can be blunt without realizing it. They need freedom to operate. They don't like teamwork and will do better on their own or in a leadership role. It's a good idea to have them work on individual projects whenever possible and give them credit for how they took the lead to resolve a challenging situation.

The Excited Enthusiasts enjoy challenges, debates, and confrontation. They are excited to start new projects and are very good at "lighting the fire" at the beginning of projects. They may not be as good as finishing what they have started, though, and for this, they would need a team. It's not a good idea to assign them to individual projects, although their motivation to take what may seem to be impossible upon themselves can be misleading. Always assign the excited enthusiastic to start new projects. They will get the team excited and create that spark for you.

The Reliable Members are slower paced and team focused. They need routines, and structure gives them peace of mind. Teamwork is perfect for them, and they are good at taking tasks upon themselves that were initiated by others. Some may be more analytical, others may be more detail oriented, but the reliable members compose the bulk of the team and they assist group leaders and the excited enthusiasts to bring their vision into fruition.

In summary, these different types of team members are important to understand in order to realize how to assign work and what to expect from each team member. It is also important in order to provide support to the team as a whole and to its members individually, helping them to succeed and excel. Once you understand the types, building your perfect team will be easy!

Misunderstandings and poor communication.
It amazes me time and time again how the vast majority of interpersonal conflict and difficulty involve so much misunderstanding. I have sat so many times in front of two or more people, all meaning well but reading the other completely wrong. Misunderstandings are usually the result of poor communication, and on top of that, we also hear in our head all of the meaning that we assign to our interactions, as discussed previously. The result? A big mish-mash of subjective information, poor communication, misunderstandings, and conflict.

Misunderstandings are problematic, because they very quickly lead to mistakes, missed deadlines, and confusion regarding project directions, and this may lead to frustration as a result, and a tremendous red-shift effect. Misunderstanding and lack of clarity always go hand in hand. When instructions aren't clearly communicated, updates and status reports aren't shared right away. When there are unclear roles or rules, misunderstandings happen, conflict arises, and people red shift from each other.

Misunderstandings are somewhat different from miscommunications. Miscommunication happens when people exchange information without clearly understanding each another. This can result in misinterpreted facts and details, which can cause one team member to head one direction while another is working in an entirely different direction. When the team members realize that miscommunication has taken place, it causes them to red shift from each other, feel angry and frustrated, and of course they each swear by their own understanding of the directions or information.

Another source of misunderstandings that cause a red shift is non-responsiveness. This is an ongoing issue that many organizations deal with. It stems from a very small, one-on-one interaction and can lead to tremendous damage to big organizations. Non-responsiveness occurs when colleagues or managers request information on any level. A person who asks for information over and over again and awaits a response may feel the other party is being intentionally uncommunicative and deliberately hurting their ability to perform their job. This can create an acute red-shift effect, as people feel that their job or professional standing is at risk as a result. Even if the non-responsiveness is due to an oversight or another benign cause, a person may assign a meaning of deliberateness or malice where there is none.

Different communication styles.
People communicate differently for many reasons: cultural diversity, personal style, personality traits, and more. Some people are more introverted in their communication but others may be very direct. It's always hard for us to deal with

someone who's different than we are, and when it comes to different communication styles, we struggle even more. It's worth noting that sending an e-mail to resolve a misunderstanding or interpersonal conflict can have the exact opposite effect and can actually cause a tremendous red shift. This is because e-mails lack the interpersonal component of a face-to-face conversation. As misinterpretation often occurs with written documents, an e-mail in this situation may even deepen the misunderstanding.

> **Dr. Rozen Says:**
> Tunnel vision is a narrow perception of an interpersonal situation that we are involved in, based on various psychological biases that impact the meaning we assign to the interaction and to our reaction as a result. Peripheral vision allows a broader perspective and creates a blue shift effect

Conflict Avoidance vs. Healthy Confrontation
Individuals who consistently, and perhaps inappropriately, prefer to do anything rather than deal face-to-face with another coworker may have a problem with avoiding conflict, and this is a red-shift action.

It's true that most of us would like to avoid conflict as much as possible. In some cases, efforts to avoid conflict may even be fitting and effective. In most cases though, avoiding conflict only contributes to the problem and prevents it from being resolved. So it's important to know the appropriate uses of avoidance as a conflict-management mode and to understand how personality dynamics influence this choice, as this will enable us to avoid a red-shift effect and to deal with conflict more successfully.

In company cultures where issues are swept under the table by both employees and managers, a red-shift dynamic is created, and the company culture descends. Why? Well, when issues are swept under the table, resentment becomes more likely, and there is often no true opportunity to clarify the situation and move forward. The rule of thumb is that conflict avoidance creates conflict! So the price for conflict avoidance is high: further conflict, escalation, damage to teamwork and to productivity, and so on—a true red-shift impact. But why does conflict avoidance happen? In truth, there are a lot of reasons.

- Lack of self-confidence
- Lack of trust in the other person's potential reaction

- A previous poor experience with conflict management
- Concern about disappointing or upsetting the other person
- Cultural-based conflict style (e.g., nice people do not confront other people)

Company cultures that practice conflict avoidance become descending company cultures tremendously quickly. Imagine the case where there's a lot of watercooler talk, but management knows very little. Teamwork would become problematic, insufficient, and ineffective. In order to create a blue-shift effect and turn the company culture into an ascending one, conflict avoidance should be discouraged. What should be encouraged is open, honest, respectful, and safe communications where issues can be brought up and ironed out in order to allow for teamwork to take place.

As Karl Popper, one of the most influential twentieth-century philosophers of science once eloquently stated, "All life is problem solving," and resolving conflict is undoubtedly a form of problem solving. I've often said that the best leaders are the best problem solvers—and so they don't avoid conflict! Leaders see problems as symptomatic of a broader challenge that they face. In essence, true leaders see problems as an opportunity for growth.

When conflict avoidance is manifested by employees, it is problematic enough. The problem is that often, it's the management itself that walks the path of conflict avoidance instead of tackling what needs to be tackled.

So how to avoid conflict avoidance?

1. Transparent communication.

Problem solving requires transparent communication, in which everyone's concerns and points of view are freely expressed. It's difficult it is to get to the heart of the matter quickly when people don't speak up.

Yes, communication is a fundamental necessity. That's why when those involved in the problem would rather not express themselves, fearing they may threaten their job and/or expose their own or someone else's wrongdoing, the problem-solving process becomes nearly impossible. Effective communication toward problem solving happens because of a leader's ability to facilitate an open dialogue and model that behavior in order to set the tone.

2. A platform for safe communication.

Any platform for safe communication creates an immediate blue-shift effect, because it allows people to not only express themselves but also to hear the thoughts and feelings of the other people involved. It breaks barriers, promotes empathy, and brings people closer. A platform for safe communication would typically come in the form of a well-planned and well-facilitated meeting, set either by management or by a neutral third party professional.

The goal of setting a platform for safe communication is to share information proactively. Blaming and past talk have no place in platforms for safe communication—otherwise they are not safe, and conflict may erupt. These platforms also eliminate conflict avoidance, as avoidance typically only occurs when those involved don't know what to do with the situation or feel uncomfortable in resolving it.

3. Clear rules and guidelines.

Conflict avoidance indicates confusion. When people feel confused, they prefer not to deal with it, as they don't know what to expect. If people are clear about the guidelines and they know for sure that the guidelines have not been followed by management or a fellow employee, they will be able to create a healthy confrontation. This is because they can always lean back on the clear guidelines and rely on them rather than feeling as though they're making a personal attack. It's the responsibility of any manager interested in creating an ascending company culture to make sure that everyone is clear on all expectations, guidelines, and policies.

So what is a healthy confrontation?
A healthy confrontation, which is always indicative of a blue-shift effect, adheres to four basic principles: it's proactive, it's forward looking, it's accepting, and it promotes learning.

The proactive nature of a healthy confrontation is, in a nutshell, the ability to say, "This has happened, and there is nothing we can do about what has already happened, *but* what can we do differently in the future to make sure that this does not happen again?" This completely changes the discussion, flipping it from blaming to making different choices going forward, and those choices will ultimately lead to different and better results.

The forward-looking nature of a healthy confrontation is found in the avoidance of past talk. People tend to spend a lot of energy analyzing the past, typically repeating the same negative information regarding something that has happened, and this repetition leads nowhere. That is an unhealthy practice. A healthy confrontation stands in the present and looks over to the future. The past is the past. We can engage in a brief past talk for the sake of learning but then quickly shift to the present and the future—they are at the center of our focus.

In a healthy confrontation, we are accepting of the other people involved. We can confront them about how things should be handled going forward and let them know that how things were handled in the past won't work for us, but we should be accepting of who they are and where they're coming from. So being judgmental and oppositional is a big no-no! Rapport and empathy go a long way in creating a blue-shift effect and in keeping confrontations healthy and productive.

A healthy confrontation promotes learning, too, because we are open to learning new ways of working and handling our communication with others. For a healthy confrontation to be successful, we need to be open to learn new information that involves our own conduct, understand what we can improve, and move forward.

Dr. Rozen Says:
Company cultures whereby conflict avoidance is the norm become descending company cultures because of the lack of opportunity to turn challenges into opportunities for growth. Healthy confrontations create a blue shift effect and contribute to an ascending company culture.

ASSUMING VS. COURAGEOUS CONVERSATIONS

We all sometimes face difficult conversations that need to be carefully handled. And we all dread them! We can call those *courageous conversations*, because they often require so much courage to handle. On a personal level, this can be a conversation with your spouse, your parent, your sibling, or friend. In the work environment, this can be a much-dreaded conversation with your boss, your colleague, or even a client.

Whether at work or at home, the implications and concerns are quite similar: loss of the recipient, creation of hostility, detachment, loss of interest altogether, having to deal with a highly emotional reaction that will be hard for us to manage, tears, anger, yelling, and perhaps accusations. Who knows? Such a courageous conversation may develop in many different ways, and that's part of what frightens us. We know that we need to have it, that what we have to say has to be said, but we also know that we are taking a risk—a big risk. And who knows what the reaction may be and how this conversation may end?

On the other hand, there is the other option: avoidance. We might have tried that option before, even several times. The reality is that during those times when a courageous conversation needs to take place, avoidance will only lead to a deterioration of the situation.

Here are some questions that you may want to ask yourself in order to evaluate if a courageous conversation needs to take place:

- How severe is the situation that I am looking to address?
- What are my possible risks?
- What are my possible gains?
- Who is my recipient? What is his or her personality like? How is he or she likely to respond?

Some people, when handling a courageous conversation, are so concerned about the reaction to the message that they are looking to convey and so concerned about the consequences, that they do what is called *avoidant communication*. That means that while they do have the courageous conversation, realizing that it needs to take place, they deliver the message in such a foggy, obscure manner, that what had to be said is not really said clearly, and the recipient is quite likely not to really get it. And that makes all the heartache and worry over the conversation pointless!

Here are your five golden rules to make sure that your message comes across, and in the clearest and most effective way:

1. Make sure that everything you say is accurate and backed up by facts.
2. Make sure to check the accuracy of information ahead of time.
3. Avoid unnecessary repetition or expansion with more and more adjectives, as this can lead to a lack of accuracy. Stick to the facts.
4. Practice ahead of time, many times, as preparation for your meeting.

5. Remain calm, and be prepared to receive feedback from the recipient as well. The recipient will likely have some feedback for you, too, and as much as you want to be listened to and respected in what you are looking to convey, your recipient may also have something to say and perhaps a perspective that you might not have considered. So don't only convey messages but also be an attentive recipient yourself—act as you hope the recipient will act!

According to the Cambridge Dictionary, assuming is "to accept something as true without question or proof." We tend to assume simply because we sometimes have no choice. We have to process large amounts of data about many people and many interactions every day, and we need to explain them to ourselves so that we can ascribe meaning and take subsequent actions. There is simply no possible way for us to have proof for every single action and every single interaction, and so in order to move forward and make decisions, we assume things. There are ten main biases when it comes to assuming. This is how they impact the way we interact with others and may lead to red-shift-oriented dynamics.

Assuming Bias No 1: The False Consensus Effect.
We talked a bit about the false consensus effect before, but it applies to the discussion on assumptions really well. Do you ever assume that other people believe something, simply

because you do? If so, you may be suffering from the false consensus effect. In other words, you overestimate how much your own beliefs are typical to other people as well. It's actually very common, and no, it's not just arrogance! Most people tend to assume that their own opinions, preferences, and values are normal and that others should think the same way, too. This false consensus can be problematic, though, because it ties directly into our own subjective narratives about the people around us, about ourselves, and about how we interpret the behavior and actions of others.

Why does the false consensus effect happen?

There are lots of potential answers to the question of why this happens, but one of the possible causes of the false consensus effect involves what is known as the *availability heuristic*, or to put it simpler, a mental shortcut that relies on immediate examples that come to mind. Take decision making as an example. When you are trying to make a decision, a number of related events or situations might immediately spring to the forefront of your thoughts. Since they were the first things you thought of, you judge that since those events are more frequent, they are also more possible than others. You give greater credence to this information, and as a result, you tend to overestimate the probability of something similar happening in the future.

Put simply, when you are trying to determine if other people share your beliefs, you might immediately think of people who are the most similar to you (such as your family and friends), and it's very likely that they do share many things in common with you. Because these examples come to mind so readily, you might be led to believe that a higher proportion of the population also shares those same qualities with you.

An availability heuristic as above, though, is not the only reason that a false consensus could happen. Researchers have suggested that there are three main reasons.

1. Similarity in immediate environment.
   Our family and friends are more likely to be similar to us and share many of the same beliefs and behaviors. Since our primary interactions are with these people, we tend to overestimate how much other people will also behave in the same way. In other words, because those close to us behave in a certain way, we assume that everyone else (or at least, a big proportion of them) does too.
2. It serves the purpose of our self-esteem.
   Believing that other people think and act the same way we do can be beneficial to our self-esteem. In order to feel good about ourselves, we tend to think that other people are just like us, or, at least, we don't like to think of ourselves as different.
3. We know our own attitudes the best!
   We are the most familiar with our own attitudes and beliefs. Since these ideas are always at the forefront of our minds, we're more likely to notice when other

people share similar attitudes, leading us to overestimate just how common these beliefs really are.

There are some factors that can increase the impact of the false consensus effect too, such as:

- When the matter in question is of great importance to the individual.
- When the behavior, attitude, or belief seems to be directly linked to a specific situation.
- When people are very confident that their point of view is correct or at least more valid than another's.

The effect is also stronger when we are very sure that our beliefs, opinions, or ideas are right. For example, if you're absolutely 100 percent convinced that passing a certain law will reduce the amount of crime in your community, you will be more likely to believe that the majority of other voters in your town will also support that law.

What's more, the false consensus effect tends to be more prevalent in situations where we are heavily invested in the issue at hand. In order words, if you really care about something, you are more likely to think others care, too. If you are very concerned about the environment, for example, you will probably be more likely to overestimate the number of people who are also very concerned about environmental issues.

Assuming Bias No. 2: The Ultimate Attribution Error.
The ultimate attribution error is a subtype of the fundamental attribution error (FAE) that we discussed earlier. The ultimate attribution error occurs when negative behavior in one's own group is explained away as circumstantial, but negative behavior among outsiders is believed to be evidence of flaws in character. It's also the belief that positive acts performed by in-group members are a result of their personality, whereas negative behaviors by the same member are thought of as rare and a result of situational factors

A classic example is the person who doesn't return your call. You could go the usual route and think, "He is an inconsiderate slob and my parents were right years ago when they said I should have dropped him as a friend." But the fundamental attribution error would remind you that there might very well be other reasons why this person hasn't called you back. Maybe he's going through major issues in his life. Maybe he's traveling for work. Maybe he honestly forgot. (Maybe before you get all hot and bothered, you should check the obituaries, though if you're really the resentful sort, even death may not be enough to mollify you.)

Closely related to the FAE is the tendency we all have to take things too personally. Maybe you could call this the fundamental selfishness error or the "all about me" effect. This describes the everyday experience of encountering people who don't treat you as you believe you deserve to be treated. The feeling we have of being disrespected is so common that we've shortened the word to "dissed." Imagine someone says something that you feel belittles you, or ignores you, or talks about food when you want to talk about sports. You've been dissed! Doesn't that person know who you are?

However, if we all take a step back to recognize and accept the fundamental attribution error, we will feel dissed far less often. Most people are good and decent, subject to the same difficulties in life as you are. When they ignore us, don't say thank you when we hold a door open for them, step on our feet and don't apologize, or make nasty comments about our mothers, we must remember that they are simply fellow sufferers. Maybe they are just having a bad day.

Assuming Bias No. 3: Self-Justification.
Self-justification is the tendency to defend and bolster the status quo. For example, existing social arrangements tend to be preferred and alternatives disparaged—sometimes even at the expense of individual and collective self-interest. We self-justify in order to avoid cognitive dissonance, which means dealing with conflicting beliefs, values, or attitudes. We don't want to deal with internal conflict or cognitive dissonance, and so we find ways to self-justify why we chose one value or belief over another. So how do we actually do it? We have a rather practical mechanism (which obviously leads to a bias) whereby we convince ourselves that we can rationalize our decision or behavior in the aftermath. We do this by screening any contrary data and leave in our minds only that which would support the

decision we made. In other words, we pick and choose which bits of data we pay attention to and which to discard.

Assuming Bias No. 4: The Trait Ascription Bias.
The trait ascription bias is the tendency for people to view themselves as relatively variable in terms of personality, behavior, and mood while viewing others as much more predictable in their personal traits across different situations. More specifically, it's a tendency to describe one's own behavior in terms of situational factors while preferring to describe another's behavior by ascribing fixed dispositions to their personality. This could occur because a person's own internal state is more readily observable and available to them than those of others.

This attributional bias intuitively plays a role in the formation and maintenance of stereotypes and prejudice, combined with the negativity effect. Trait ascription and trait-based models of personality remain contentious in modern psychology and social science research, but trait ascription bias refers to the situational and dispositional evaluation and description of traits on a personal level. A similar bias on a group level is called the out-group homogeneity bias.

Taking this back to the workplace, we can sometimes be quick to point out the flaws in others that are causing a slowdown in their business, but rarely do we see these same things in ourselves. We see the variables in our own personality but find those of our business competitors quite predictable. We feel we can handle a variety of situations with flexibility, and if it doesn't work out, it has to be because of something beyond our control, but we don't allow the same flexibility for our competitors. Ascribing traits to others for the same behavior we show, while laying the blame for the behavior firmly on them, is a trait ascription bias, and we are all guilty of doing this at one time or another. However, when it becomes a common thing and our business reflects this, then it's time to consider why we are this way and what we can do to change it.

A good example is a business owner who angers easily, tends to take it out on his employees, and at times his customers. While he calls this a reasonable misunderstanding when it pertains to himself, he considers it neurotic in other business owners and accuses them of a lack of discipline and cooperation. There is always a reason for one's own behavior that is quite understandable, but the business owner accuses others of having unfortunate, deep-rooted personality traits.

Assuming Bias No. 5: The Selective Perception Bias.
The selective perception bias is the tendency to select, categorize, and analyze data from our environment in order to create meaning while blocking or tuning out any data that contradicts our expectations. This means that we focus on certain stimulation, information, or data, and block or disregard others. We filter it.

So why is this so tricky? Simply put, each of us has a schema: a collection of ideas, experiences, and associations that we bring to a situation, and we have a tendency to open ourselves to information far more readily when it fits in easily with what is already there. This means that information gathering, an important part of the decision-making process, can be skewed in ways that harm the process. At the most primitive level, when I own a red car, I see red cars everywhere, causing me to believe that there are now more red cars on the road. That is not going to affect very much, so it's not a problem. However, if I'm a manager and I have recently read an article on wastefulness in the production process, if I need to cut costs somewhere, that is likely to be my focus, possibly causing me to miss some more important aspects of cost cutting. So selective perception can harm the decision-making process, cutting us off from observing viable alternatives.

Assuming Bias No. 6: The Projection Bias.
As individuals trapped inside our minds 24-7, it's often difficult for us to project outside the bounds of our own consciousness and preferences. We've already clarified that we tend to assume that most people think just like us, though there may be no justification for it. This cognitive shortcoming often leads to the false consensus bias that we discussed earlier. It's a bias where we overestimate how typical and normal we are and assume that a consensus exists on matters when there may be none. Moreover, it can also lead to members of a radical or fringe group wrongly assuming that more people on the outside agree with them, or the exaggerated confidence one has when predicting the winner of an election or a sports match.

Assuming Bias No. 7: The Self-Serving Bias.
The self-serving bias refers to a tendency for people to take personal responsibility for their desirable outcomes yet externalize responsibility for their undesirable outcomes. In other words, "What I did well was down to me, but what I did poorly was the fault of others." There are a variety of explanations for this attribution bias. Although researchers have historically pitted cognitive and motivational explanations against one another, these processes often work in tandem, leading people to conclude that they are responsible for the desirable but not the undesirable outcomes.

So if the team did great and the client is happy, you attribute it to your own awesomeness (internal attribution). But if the team didn't do as well and the client is unhappy, you attribute it to certain team members and feel upset with them (external attribution).

Assuming Bias No. 8: The Transparency Bias.
This refers to the feeling that our emotions are transparent to others, when in fact they are not, or at least not as much as we think they are. This is closely related to the illusion of transparency: we always know what we mean by our words, and so we expect others to know it, too. Reading our own writing is a great example, as the intended interpretation falls easily into place, guided by our knowledge of what we really meant. In this instance, it's hard to empathize with someone who must interpret blindly, guided only by our written words. None of this means, of course, that our thoughts and feelings are totally

impenetrable to others. Nevertheless the illusion of transparency is worth bearing in mind, as it affects so much of our everyday life and helps explain arguments that begin with, "But I thought it was obvious how I felt…"

Assuming Bias No. 9: The Actor-Observer Bias.
The actor-observer bias is the tendency, when examining the behavior of others, to overemphasize the influence of their personality and underemphasize the influence of their situation. This is coupled with the opposite tendency for the self, in that one's explanations for their own behaviors overemphasize their situation and underemphasize the influence of their personality. The actor-observer bias, then, refers to the fact that we base our behavior on the implications that we make about our behavior and the behavior of others. The attributions we make depend directly on whether we are the actor or the observer.

Assuming Bias No. 10: The Dunning-Kruger Bias.
The Dunning-Kruger bias happens when people are incompetent in the strategies they adopt to achieve success and satisfaction, and as a result they suffer a dual burden: Not only do they reach erroneous conclusions and make unfortunate choices, but their incompetence robs them of the ability to realize it. Instead, they are left with the mistaken impression that they are doing just fine. The Dunning-Kruger effect is the illusion of competence that comes from ignorance. We see something, and we say to ourselves: "I could do that, how hard can it be?"

And we say it without fully understanding the skill and experience required for mastery. The Dunning-Kruger effect can be a good thing, too, because it gives us a false sense of confidence to try something new. After all, without the naïve optimism of the Dunning-Kruger effect, we'd probably give up on a lot of things without even trying.

There are a lot biases that we use to make assumptions, and these can all have an effect on the conversations we have. If we step away from making assumptions and their red-shift effect on us, we initiate a courageous conversation. These conversations mean that we can be successful in the handling of a difficult situation. Rather than making assumptions about why things happened, we confront the other person, ready to talk and ready to listen.

> **Dr. Rozen Says:**
> Assuming things about the other, or about an interaction with the other, is heavily impacted by cognitive biases, creates a red shift effect and leads to a descending company culture. Courageous conversations create a blue shift effect because they create a healthy dialogue and are common in ascending company cultures.

THE ONE-SOLUTION APPROACH VS. THE MULTIPLE-SOLUTIONS APPROACH

Having one preconceived solution to any type of conflict is problematic. It's problematic because it very quickly leads to an impasse, and impasse leads to escalation. People who handle conflicts with one preconceived solution to the problem that is being faced, whatever that problem may be, would typically swear by their solution. They believe that their solution is the only reasonable, possible, or good solution, and that all they need to do is to convince the other side that their solution is the ultimate one. The problem is that often, that other side is not so convinced, to say the least, and in fact, they may be walking around with their own preconceived solution as well. From there, the road to impasse and escalation is pretty short. In fact, this is a stairway to conflict, and it's a fast lane for sure. This leads to red-shift dynamics, because if each of the parties has one preconceived solution, there can be no dialogue.

Typically, in red-shifted situations where people have one preconceived solution, two types of problem categories may arise: escalation and destructive avoidance.

Escalation

Escalation happens with the decrease and withdrawal of dialogue, and dialogue is truly not possible when each side is stuck in their own preconceived solution, because they are locked. They are not really open to listening to the other, and they constantly shift to convincing the other about why their solution is the one that truly works. This would lead to much frustration on both sides and, as a result, to quick escalation.

> **Typical Scenario:**
>
> **Susan:** There is one solution to the problems within our team. And one solution only.
>
> **Mark:** Really? What is it?
>
> **Susan:** To get rid of Frank. Once he is out, we can definitely get the work done.
>
> **Mark:** Isn't that a little extreme?
>
> **Susan:** No, believe me. There is no other way.

Destructive Avoidance

Destructive avoidance happens when people are so stuck in their preconceived solutions, and they get so frustrated when their solutions are not accepted that they decide to completely avoid the other person. This is typical of descending company cultures and is at the far end of the scale in terms of the severity of a red-shift effect. Destructive avoidance is aimed to accomplish the following:

1. Deliberately fail the other person.
2. Stating to management that this person is impossible to work with.

3. Placing oneself above the other, as if to say that one has the power to make the other person nonexistent. This sends a message about how unimportant they are and how valuable and dedicated the person who uses the destructive avoidance believes themselves to be.

Generating options, then, is a great blue-shift action, because it gives the parties hope and a sense of being unstuck. It amazes me time and time again how people become incredibly centered around their one preconceived solution and will fiercely fight against the one preconceived solution of the other. Both parties simply don't consider that there may be other options as well, but the process of generating options for a possible solution within a department or team is extremely important. This is because the dynamics of brainstorming creates a sense of teamwork and allows a feeling of ownership once a solution is achieved. I believe that through training leaders, departments, and teams to generate options rather than getting stuck in one preconceived solution is essential for creating and maintaining ascending company cultures.

Knowing this, it's clear that one of the most effective strategies you can learn as a manager is to create a solutions-oriented environment that encourages employees to think through challenges and create appropriate solutions as a team. To do so, leaders should follow these steps.

1. Create a safe environment. When people are fearful of the consequences of making mistakes, it's only

logical that they're reluctant to volunteer solutions. Environments where errors are criticized or ridiculed aren't conducive to constructive problem solving, as people are afraid to speak up. After all, nobody wants to make a fool of themselves, and nobody wants to get into trouble for saying the wrong thing! Create a safe environment where people can confidently ask questions and suggest solutions by always maintaining your composure, being patient, and remaining objective. Make it clear that everybody on the team will be treated with the same amount of respect and that inappropriate, judgmental responses won't be tolerated. By setting these ground rules, you send the message that it's OK to not have all the answers, and it's OK to make mistakes during this learning process.

2. Explain that problems are challenges. People who are worried about making mistakes rarely see problems as anything but obstacles. That's why it's crucial you teach your employees that problems are actually challenges that contain learning opportunities. By getting answers or coming up with solutions themselves, employees can deepen their knowledge and skills, enhance their performance, and even increase their productivity. At the same time, by showing your team the positive side of challenges, you can help them become less intimidated when problems arise.

3. Give them ownership. In order for your team members to be fully invested in an outcome, they need to feel a

sense of ownership for the challenge. That's why it's imperative that everybody on the team knows exactly what the problem is, what's at stake, and what important factors could influence the outcome. Give them the chance to make it personal, since it will encourage them to work harder to find solutions.

4. Promote equality. Some people are more forthcoming with questions and ideas than others. Others have the natural inclination to step in and lead. Though this can be good, those who are more reserved can have equally good thoughts. Promote equality by giving everybody on the team a chance to speak out about the problem as a whole as well as about any aspect of the challenge that pertains specifically to his or her area of expertise.

5. Encourage questions. As your team learns to find solutions, it's crucial that you encourage them to ask questions that will help them think through the challenge. Make it clear that there's no such thing as a stupid question. Teach them to try a variety of lines of questioning until they hit upon the one that will lead them to a solution.

6. Provide resources. Instead of providing all of the answers yourself, show your team where they can find the answers to their questions for themselves. Whether it's contacting somebody in another department or researching a company database, empowering your

employees with practical resources will promote their confidence.
7. Put it together. Once your employees have asked the right questions and found sufficient answers, it's time for them to put it all together and draw conclusions. During this process, it's important to continue to encourage input from everybody on the team so that the solution eventually decided on meets with everyone's approval.

By teaching your team to find solutions to challenges and subsequently encouraging them to do so on a regular basis, you can help them become confident, creative problem solvers. And that in turn can result in enhanced productivity and an improved bottom line.

> **Dr. Rozen says:**
> The Multiple Options Approach is an options-generating approach which is the opposite of the One Solution Approach. It encourages blue shift oriented dynamics, and it is an essential part of problem solving in ascending company cultures.

THE BEST TRICK FOR BRINGING OPPOSING TEAM MEMBERS TOGETHER

People spend a lot of time blaming others, or themselves for that matter, for how a problem occurred, and how it later developed. Typically their blame or guilt would be based on their narrative and perception of the situation, which are, of course, completely subjective. Since the perception of the conflict is in their mind, the whole concept of who is to blame and why, is in their mind as well. The truth is, people spend a lot of time thinking about who is "really to blame," but this is actually not very relevant, and it's definitely not helpful to resolving the conflict.

Every time we blame someone for the conflict that we are dealing with, we are making a red-shift-oriented choice. If we feel that the other person is to blame and they feel that we are to blame, we have drifted miles from each other. How can we bridge that? How can we come to any kind of understanding? Externalization of the problem releases us from the habit of searching for who is at fault, and the goal is to alleviate the whole burden of fault finding. It takes the edge off blaming and guilt and helps people unite in light of the problem.

Our lives consist of a series of stories or narratives that we tell ourselves, in which we assign meaning to our experiences. There is no such thing as "what actually happened." There are just different narratives of different people. The truth is that you cannot really argue with someone that her narrative is "wrong" and your narrative is "right." You would be surprised to find just how much time and energy people spend in doing exactly that, but they become frustrated when they get nowhere. So rather than arguing over whose narrative is the "right" one, externalizing a problem allows you to discover a third narrative: it's not me, it's not you, but it's *this*. Externalizing the problem in this way is the oldest trick in the book, and it creates an immediate blue-shift effect.

And when I say *this*, here is a partial list of what *this* can stand for. These are the sorts of things that can cause two fellow employees to fall into the black and sticky pit of workplace conflict when they would have gotten along great in any other circumstances.

- Unclear expectations regarding the project/task.
- Changes in management.
- Changes within company/department.
- Working with a difficult client.
- Highly challenging goals/deadlines.
- Challenging office environment.
- Unpredictable policies.
- Insufficient resources.
- Stress.
- Misunderstanding.
- Distribution of workload.
- Economic pressures.
- Politics within department/company.

So what you are actually doing when you externalize the cause for your conflict is reversing its internalization. Typically, the problems you are dealing with have been internalized and are embedded in the accounts that people share. When problems disguise themselves as truth, they prevent alternatives, exceptions, and possibilities from coming to light. The problem's existence is perceived as a given, which is a red-shift state. You want to shift from that to externalizing the problem, which is a blue-shift action that will bring you closer. Together, you can brainstorm how to deal with "the problem."

How to Externalize the Problem that Led to the Conflict
1. **Separate the person from the problem.**

Our rule of thumb is that we should view problems as separate from people. Based on that separation, we use the technique of externalization to distinguish between the person and the problem that they present to us. It's very important to refer to problems as nouns and thus as separate objectified entities. Once you have separated the person from the problem, there can no longer be any anger. After all, would you be angry at people who limp simply because they limp? Of course you wouldn't. They have a problem, and it's not their fault. The same can be applied to almost any situation. Separating the person from the problem can easily lead to creative problem solving.

> **Typical Scenario:**
>
> **Mary:** Dayna, we both have a problem. All those changes in the company caused a problem in our teamwork.
>
> **Dayna:** Yes, you are right, there is really a problem.
>
> **Mary:** We have to figure out how to tackle it. We have to figure out ways to work around the situation in the company and see how we can make it work.
>
> **Dayna:** I totally agree. Those changes are driving me nuts too.

2. Personify the problem and attribute oppressive intentions and tactics to it.

When you use externalizing language, you may want to also ascribe actions, intentions, and so forth as part of the "problem." For example, "It seems like changes in the office pushed us one against the other."

> **Typical Scenario:**
>
> **Jim:** The dynamics between our team members is out of sync. It is really failing us.
>
> **Debra:** Of course, it's impossible to work this way.
>
> **Jim:** I really feel that we are all capable of working better together. This dynamics is something that we should all work towards changing.
>
> **Debra:** Yes, I absolutely agree with you.

Benefits of externalizing the problem:

1. Decreases unproductive conflict between people, including disputes over who is responsible for the problem.
2. Undermines the sense of failure that has developed for many people in response to the continuing existence of the problem, despite their attempts to resolve it.
3. Paves the way for people to cooperate with each other, to unite in a struggle against the problem, and to escape its influence in their lives.

4. Opens up new possibilities for people to take action. From the problem and its influence, people can get back their lives and relationships.
5. Frees people to take a lighter, more effective, and less stressed approach to serious problems.
6. Presents options for dialogue about the problem.

Through externalizing conversations we put into practice the idea that people and problems are separate. Externalization allows narrative therapists a space in which they can work to understand problems without seeing the people themselves as problematic or pathological. As problems are externalized, we begin to inhabit a world where, rather than being problematic in and of themselves, people have relationships with problems. When told in the context of an externalizing conversation, people's stories almost always become less blame- and guilt-ridden, and hence less restrictive.

> **Dr. Rozen Says:**
> Externalization of problems allows team members to work together towards solving their differences without blaming each other. It's an effective blue shift action and it's an integral part of conflict management in ascending company cultures.

Defusing Bombs

Controlling our impulsive red-shift actions and moving toward blue-shift ones by handling conflict effectively requires us to let go of our impulsive conflict-management techniques and to use our emotional intelligence. The problem is that we differ greatly from each other, not only in *how* we address conflict but also in *when* we prefer to address it. Our first reaction to any situation is generally emotional. In times of conflict, this emotional reaction can take over and control the process. What's more, there's an instinctive fight-or-flight physical response to escalating stress. But we can use these emotional, instinctive reactions to our benefit if we use them with intelligence. Our emotional intelligence describes our ability to understand our emotions and the emotions of others and to recognize those emotions as they surface. The goal is to use that increased awareness to more effectively manage our interactions with others, especially in stressful situations.

A situation where intense anger is involved, whether regarding a specific instance or on an ongoing basis, could be described as a bomb—and like all bombs, it needs to be defused! Just like in the battlefield, good soldiers defuse bombs because they realize their potential devastating damage—and of course, they don't want to be blown up with it!

But how do you defuse a bomb in the workplace?

There are four main principles to defusing a bomb in the workplace. Remember, your goal in defusing the bomb is to create a blue-shift effect—bringing people together instead of blowing them apart. By sticking to the following principles, you should reach that goal:

1. Timing

When defusing the bomb, the rule of thumb is *don't touch the pot when it's hot!* In other words, never defuse a bomb when someone is very mad—it'll only make things worse. Let that person cool off while sending messages that indicate empathy and collaboration. Then carefully pick your time to talk. Don't do it in the hallway or when the person is under stress. If your timing is off, the bomb will explode, and you will go down with it!

2. Empathy

Angry people react poorly when they feel criticized or teamed up against, but they react really well when they feel empathized with. Empathy goes a long way in defusing bombs; people feel positively toward those who understand them; and as a result, they blue shift toward them. Empathy also has a soothing effect and goes a long way in defusing problematic, anger-based situations.

3. Externalization

Don't forget to externalize the issue and separate the person from the problem. Avoid laying blame. Instead, define the external problem and team up with the angry person to think how, together, you can tackle it.

4. Collaboration

Remember, you're a team! You're on the same side, not opposing sides. Simply saying that is not enough, so show it. Include other people in the thinking process, and show them that you're *with* them not against them. Understand where they're coming from, and then together come up with solutions about how things can be done differently. In other words, blue shift toward them even before they blue shift toward you!

> **Dr. Rozen Says:**
> Touching the pot when it's hot will never lead to effectively handle a heated situation. The key is to move from red shift dynamics of interaction, to blue shift dynamics.

5

A Few Words of Summary

Engagement, productivity, and success do not happen out of nowhere. They are the result of an ascending, well-developed company culture that fosters these values and works hard to implement them in the everyday dynamics of the company.
Conflict-saturated company cultures and decreased engagement are a sign for management that it's time to roll up sleeves and get to work. The good news is that creating ascending company cultures—in which people blue shift toward one another

and engagement, motivation, and productivity increase—is not a matter of luck or miracle. There is a system to it. Once the system is used, with much care and attention, the fruit of success will surely come, and both company and employees will reap the benefits. Remember, we all want to do well; we are just very different.

Yours truly,
Dr. Michelle Rozen

6

Test Yourself: Does Your Company Demonstrate Characteristics of an Ascending Company Culture or a Descending Company Culture?

So is your company ascending or descending? Find out by taking part in this simple quiz.

Rate the following statements from 0 to 10, with 0 being "not at all true" and 10 being "entirely true."

1. The teams under my management work well together.
   0   1   2   3   4   5   6   7   8   9   10

2. Employees in my organization/unit are engaged.
   0   1   2   3   4   5   6   7   8   9   10

3. Employees in my organization/unit are happy with their work here.
   0   1   2   3   4   5   6   7   8   9   10

4. Employees in my organization/unit work out their differences effectively.
   0   1   2   3   4   5   6   7   8   9   10

5. Employees in my organization/unit are clear about roles, rules, and expectations.
   0   1   2   3   4   5   6   7   8   9   10

6. Employees in my organization/unit demonstrate a high level of productivity.
   0   1   2   3   4   5   6   7   8   9   10

7. I don't see any reason for concern in terms of employee turnover.
   0   1   2   3   4   5   6   7   8   9   10

8. There is great deal of opportunity for growth in my company.
   0   1   2   3   4   5   6   7   8   9   10

9. We are adaptable in terms of our ability to handle competition.
   0   1   2   3   4   5   6   7   8   9   10

10. My organization/unit has a good culture of giving and receiving feedback.
    0   1   2   3   4   5   6   7   8   9   10

11. I am happy with the level of teamwork in my company.
    0   1   2   3   4   5   6   7   8   9   10

12. I am happy with my employees' abilities to work with diverse personalities.
    0   1   2   3   4   5   6   7   8   9   10

13. Employees in my company do well at handling difficult conversations with other employees.
    0   1   2   3   4   5   6   7   8   9   10

14. There is a low level of unhealthy conflict in my company.
    0   1   2   3   4   5   6   7   8   9   10

15. Conflict avoidance is not common in my company.
    0   1   2   3   4   5   6   7   8   9   10

16. Assuming things about other employees is not common in our organization.
    0   1   2   3   4   5   6   7   8   9   10

17. We have a plethora of safe communication platforms.
    0   1   2   3   4   5   6   7   8   9   10

18. There is a high level of tolerance for different communication styles.
    0   1   2   3   4   5   6   7   8   9   10

Take a look at your answers. A high grade for each answer indicates that there is no need for concern in that respect. A middle or low grade indicates an area of concern. What areas do you need to work on? Remember, problems are an opportunity for growth, and realizing what they are is the first step. You have just taken it!

Works Consulted

Abele, J. (2011). Bringing minds together. Harvard Business Review (July/August): 86-93.

Abernathy, W. (1997). "Balanced scorecards make teamwork a reality". *The Journal for Quality and Participation* (November/December): 58-59.

Adler, P., C. Hecksher and L. Prusak. (2011). "Building a collaborative enterprise". *Harvard Business Review* (July/August): 94-101.

Adler, P. S. and C. X. Chen. (2011). "Combining creativity and control: Understanding individual motivation in large-scale collaborative creativity". *Accounting, Organizations and Society* 36(2): 63-85.

Amason, A. C. (1996). "Distinguishing the effects of functional and dysfunctional conflict on strategic decision making: Resolving a paradox for top management teams". *The Academy of Management Journal* 39(1): 123-148

Ancona, D., H. Bresman and K. Kaeufer. (2002). "The comparative advantage of X-teams". *MIT Sloan Management Review* (Spring): 33-39.

Ancona, D. G. (1990). "Outward bound: Strategies for team survival in an organization". *The Academy of Management Journal* 33(2): 334-365

Ancona, D. G. and D. F. Caldwell. (1992). "Bridging the boundary: External activity and performance in organizational teams". *Administrative Science Quarterly* 37(4): 634-665.

Arentson, R. W. (1947). "Team accounting". *N.A.C.A. Bulletin* (May 15): 1149-1154.

Asimov, E. (2008). Wine's pleasures: Are they all in your head? *New York Times*, May 7, 2008.

Baker, E. M. (1999). *Scoring a Whole in One: People in Enterprise Playing in Concert (Best Management Practices)*. Crisp Publications.

Baldwin, W. (1982). "This is the answer". *Forbes* (July 5): 50-52.

Balkundi, P. and D. A. Harrison. (2006). "Ties, leaders, and time in teams: Strong inference about network structure's effects on team viability and performance". *The Academy of Management Journal* 49(1): 49-68, 2006.

Erratum (2006): Ties, leaders, and time in teams: Strong inference about network structure's effects on team viability and performance. *The Academy of Management Journal* 49(4): 630.

Balcetis, E., & Dunning, D. (2006). "See what you want to see: Motivational influences on visual perception". *Journal of Personality and Social Psychology*, 91, 2006.

Banker, R. D., J. M. Field, R. G. Schroeder and K. K. Sinha. (1996). "Impact of work teams on manufacturing performance: A longitudinal field study". *The Academy of Management Journal* 39(4): 867-890.

Barrick, M. R., B. H. Bradley, A. L. Kristof-Brown and A. E. Colbert. (2007). The moderating role of top management team interdependence: Implications for real teams and working groups. *The Academy of Management Journal* 50(3): 544-557.

Barsade, S. G., A. J. Ward, J. D. F. Turner and J. A. Sonnenfeld. (2000). "To your heart's content: A model of affective diversity in top management teams". *Administrative Science Quarterly* 45(4): 802-836.

Beckman, C. M. (2006). "The influence of founding team company affiliations on firm behavior". *The Academy of Management Journal* 49(4): 741-758.

Beersma, B., J. R. Hollenbeck, S. E. Humphrey, H. Moon, D. E. Conlon and D. R. Ilgen. (2003). "Cooperation, competition, and team performance: Toward a contingency approach". *The Academy of Management Journal* 46(5): 572-590.

Belasco, D. R. (2000). "Team-up for success". *Strategic Finance* (May): 54-58, 60.

Bergstrom, K. H. (1947). "Teamwork accounting and management". *N.A.C.A. Bulletin* (January 2): 550-559.

Bettenhausen, K. and J. K. Murnighan. (1985). "The emergence of norms in competitive decision-making groups". *Administrative Science Quarterly* 30(3): 350-372.

Bettenhausen, K. L. and J. K. Murnighan. (1991). "The development of an intragroup norm and the effects of interpersonal and structural challenges". *Administrative Science Quarterly* 36(1): 20-35.

Blake, R. R. and J. S. Moulton. (1962). "The managerial grid". *Advanced Management Office Executive* 1(9).

Bonabeau, E. (2009). "Decisions 2.0: The power of collective intelligence". *MIT Sloan Management Review* (Winter): 45-52.

Boone, C., W. Van Olffen, A. Van Witteloostuijn and B. De Brabander. (2004). "The genesis of top management team diversity: Selective turnover among top management teams in Dutch newspaper publishing". *The Academy of Management Journal* 47(5): 633-656.

Boone, C., W. Van Olffen and A. Van Witteloostuijn. (2005). "Team locus-of-control composition, leadership structure, information acquisition, and financial performance: A business simulation study". *The Academy of Management Journal* 48(5): 889-909.

Bothwell, C. (2001). "Beating the odds". *Strategic Finance* (February): 46-51.

Boyett, J. H., and H. P. Conn. (1991). *Workplace 2000: The Revolution Reshaping American Business.* New York: Penguin Books USA Inc.

Brett, J., K. Behfar and M. C. Kern. (2006). "Managing multicultural teams". *Harvard Business Review* (November): 84-91.

Brett, J. M., R. Friedman and K. Behfar. (2009). "How to manage your negotiating team". *Harvard Business Review* (September): 105-109.

Brief, A. P., E. E. Umphress, J. Dietz, J. W. Burrows, R. M. Butz and L. Scholten. (2005). "Community matters: Realistic group conflict theory and the impact of diversity". *The Academy of Management Journal* 48(5): 830-844.

Browne, B. (2015). *Sys-Tao: Western Logic - Eastern Flow. An Emerging Leadership Philosophy*. Millichap Books.

Bryant, S. M., S. M. Albring and U. Murthy. (2009). "The effects of reward structure, media richness and gender on virtual teams". *International Journal of Accounting Information Systems* 10(4): 190-213.

Bucklow, M. (1966). "A new role for the work group". *Administrative Science Quarterly* 11(1): 59-78.

Buller, P. F. and C. H. Bell, Jr. (1986). "Effects of team building and goal setting on productivity: A field experiment". *The Academy of Management Journal* 29(2): 305-328.

Bunderson, J. S. (2003). "Team member functional background and involvement in management teams: Direct effects and the moderating role of power centralization". *The Academy of Management Journal* 46(4): 458-474.

Bunderson, J. S. and K. M. Sutcliffe. (2002). "Comparing alternative conceptualizations of functional diversity in management teams: Process and performance effects". *The Academy of Management Journal* 45(5): 875-893.

Burke, R. J., T. Weir and G. Duncan. (1976). "Informal helping relationships in work organizations". *The Academy of Management Journal* 19(3): 370-377.

Bush, G. P. and L. H. Hattery. (1956). "Teamwork and creativity in research". *Administrative Science Quarterly* 1(3): 361-372.

Briggs, K.C. & Isabel, B. M. (2015). The Myers-Briggs Type Indicator.

Croskerry, P., Singhal, G., Mamede, S. (2013). "Cognitive debiasing 1: origins of bias and theory of debiasing". *BMJ Qual Saf*. 22 (2): ii58-ii64.

Croskerry P. (2003). "The importance of cognitive bias in diagnosis and strategies to minimize them". *Acad. Med.* 2003; 78:775–780.

Carpenter, M. A. and J. W. Fredrickson. (2001). "Top management teams, global strategic posture, and the moderating role of uncertainty". *The Academy of Management Journal* 44(3): 533-545.

Carrison, D. and R. Walsh. (1998). *Semper Fi: Business Leadership the Marine Corps Way*.

Campbell D.T., (1994). "Systematic errors to be expected of the social scientist on the basis of a general psychology of cognitive bias". In: Blanck P.D., Ed, *interpersonal Expectations: Theory, Research, and Applications*. New York, Cambridge University Press.

Carson, J. B., P. E. Tesluk and J. A. Marrone. (2007). "Shared leadership in teams: An investigation of antecedent conditions and performance". *The Academy of Management Journal* 50(5): 1217-1234.

Carzo, R. (1963). "Some effects of organization structure on group effectiveness". *Administrative Science Quarterly* 7(4): 393-424.

Cohen, A. M. (1962). "Changing small-group communication networks". *Administrative Science Quarterly* 6(4): 443-462.

Collins, C. J. and K. D. Clark. (2003). "Strategic human resource practices, top management team social networks, and firm performance: The role of human resource practices in creating organizational competitive advantage". *The Academy of Management Journal* 46(6): 740-751.

Croskerry P. (2013). "From mindless to mindful practice -cognitive bias and clinical decision making". *Eng. Journal Med.* 368:2445-2448. June 27, 2013.

Coutu, D. and M. Beschloss. (2009). "Why teams don't work". *Harvard Business Review* (May): 98-105.

Cox, T. H., S. A. Lobel and P. L. McLeod. (1991). "Effects of ethnic group cultural differences on cooperative and competitive behavior on a group task". *The Academy of Management Journal* 34(4): 827-847.

Daniel Dana, *Managing Differences: How to Build Better Relationships at Work and Home* (2005); Barbara J. Kreisman, *Insights into Employee Motivation, Commitment and Retention* (2002).

Dahlin, K. B., L. R. Weingart and P. J. Hinds. (2005). "Team diversity and information use". *The Academy of Management Journal* 48(6): 1107-1123.

Demerath, N. J. and J. W. Thibaut. (1956). "Small groups and administrative organizations". *Administrative Science Quarterly* 1(2): 139-154.

Ditto, P. H., and Lopez, D. F. (1992). "Motivated skepticism: Use of differential decision criteria for preferred and non preferred conclusions". *Journal of Personality and Social Psychology*, 63, 1992.

Denison, D. R., S. L. Hart and J. A. Kahn. (1996). "From chimneys to cross-functional teams: Developing and validating a diagnostic model". *The Academy of Management Journal* 39(4): 1005-1023.

Dennis, A. R., J. A. Rennecker and S. Hansen. (2010). "Invisible whispering: Restructuring collaborative decision making with instant messaging". *Decision Sciences* 41(4): 845-886.

Dineen, B. R., R. A. Noe, J. D. Shaw, M. K. Duffy and C. Wiethoff. (2007). "Level and dispersion of satisfaction in teams: Using foci and social context to explain the satisfaction-absenteeism relationship". *The Academy of Management Journal* 50(3): 623-643.

Donovan, R. (2015). "Leading a successful team". *Strategic Finance* (September): 19-20.

Dooley, R. S. and G. E. Fryxell. (1999). "Attaining decision quality and commitment from dissent: The moderating effects of loyalty and competence in strategic decision-making teams". *The Academy of Management Journal* 42(4): 389-402.

Drake, A., S. Haka and S. Ravenscroft. (1998). "Incentive effects on innovation, interaction and productivity in group environments". *Advances in Management Accounting* (6): 93-112.

Drake, A. R., S. F. Haka and S. P. Ravenscroft. (1999). "Cost system and incentive structure effects on innovation, efficiency and profitability in teams. *The Accounting Review* (July): 323-345.

Druskat, V. U. and J. V. Wheeler. (2003). "Managing from the boundary: The effective leadership of self-managing work teams". *The Academy of Management Journal* 46(4): 435-457.

DuFrene, D. D. and C. M. Lehman. (2002). *Building High Performance Teams*. South-Western Educational Publishing.

Earley, P. C. (1993). "East meets west meets Mideast: Further explorations of collectivistic and individualistic work groups". *The Academy of Management Journal* 36(2): 319-348.

Earley, P. C. and E. Mosakowski. (2000). "Creating hybrid team cultures: An empirical test of transnational team functioning". *The Academy of Management Journal* 43(1): 26-49.

Edmondson, A. (1999). "Psychological safety and learning behavior in work teams". *Administrative Science Quarterly* 44(2): 350-383.

Edmondson, A. C. (2012). "Teamwork on the fly: How to master the new art of teaming". *Harvard Business Review* (April): 72-80.

Edwards K. and Smith E. E.(1996). "A disconfirmation bias in the evaluation of arguments". *Journal of Personality and Social Psychology*, 71,1996.

Evans, J. (1989). *Bias in human reasoning: causes and consequences.* Hillsdale, NJ, Erlbaum.

Ellis, A. P. J. (2006). "System breakdown: The role of mental models and transactive memory in the relationship between acute stress and team performance". *The Academy of Management Journal* 49(3): 576-589.

Elsbach, K. D., B. Brown-Saracino and F. J. Flynn. (2015). "Collaborating with creative peers". *Harvard Business Review* (October): 118-121.

Erez, M. and A. Somech. (1996). "Is group productivity loss the rule or the exception? Effects of culture and group-based motivation". *The Academy of Management Journal* 39(6): 1513-1537.

Evans, P. and B. Wolf. (2005). "Collaboration rules". *Harvard Business Review* (July/August): 96-104.

Finkelstein, S. (1992). "Power in top management teams: Dimensions, measurement, and validation". *The Academy of Management Journal* 35(3): 505-538.

Fischer, B. & A. Boynton.(2005). "Virtuoso teams". *Harvard Business Review* (July/August): 116-123.

Frisch, B. (2008). "When teams can't decide". *Harvard Business Review* (November): 121-126.

Frow, N., D. Marginson and S. Ogden. (2005). "Encouraging strategic behaviour while maintaining management control: Multi-functional project teams, budgets, and the negotiation of shared accountabilities in contemporary enterprises". *Management Accounting Research* (September): 269-292.

Furr, N. and J. H. Dyer. (2014). "Leading your team into the unknown". *Harvard Business Review* (December): 80-88.

Gardner, H. K. (2012). "Coming through when it matters most: How great teams do their best work under pressure". *Harvard Business Review* (April): 82-91.

Gardner, H. K. (2015). "Breaking down barriers to collaboration: Interaction". *Harvard Business Review* (May): 18.

Gersick, C. J. G. (1988). "Time and transition in work teams: Toward a new model of group development". *The Academy of Management Journal* 31(1): 9-41.

Gibson, C. B. (1999). "Do they do what they believe they can? Group efficacy and group effectiveness across tasks and cultures". *The Academy of Management Journal* 42(2): 138-152.

Gillenwater, P. J. (2008). "Take your new team to the top". *Journal of Accountancy* (March): 58-61.

Gilson, L., J. E. Mathieu, C. E. Shalley and T. M. Ruddy. (2005). "Creativity and standardization: Complementary or conflicting drivers of team effectiveness?" *The Academy of Management Journal* 48(3): 521-531.

Gladstein, D. L.(1984). "Groups in context: A model of task group effectiveness". *Administrative Science Quarterly* 29(4): 499-517.

Gladstein, D. L. and N. P. Reilly. (1985). "Group decision making under threat: The tycoon game". *The Academy of Management Journal* 28(3): 613-627.

Golembiewski, R. T. (1961). "Management science and group behavior: Work-unit cohesiveness". *The Journal of the Academy of Management* 4(2): 87-99.

Govindarajan, V. and A. K. Gupta. (2001). "Building an effective global business team". *MIT Sloan Management Review* (Summer): 63-71.

Grant Halvorson, H. (2014). "Get your team to do what it says it's going to do". *Harvard Business Review* (May): 82-87.

Gratton, L. and T. J. Erickson. (2007). "Eight ways to build collaborative teams". *Harvard Business Review* (November): 100-109.

Green, T. B. (1975). "An empirical analysis of nominal and interacting groups". *The Academy of Management Journal* 18(1): 63-73.

Greer, O. L., S. K Olson and M. Callison. (1992). "The key to real teamwork: Understanding the numbers". *Management Accounting* (May): 39-44.

Groysberg, B. and R. Abrahams. (2006). "Lift outs: How to acquire a high-functioning team". *Harvard Business Review* (December): 133-140.

Guttman, H. M. (2008). *Great Business Teams: Cracking the Code for Standout Performance*. New York: Wiley.

Gilovich T. (1991). *How we know what is not so: the fallibility of human reason in everyday life*. New York, NY. The Free Press.

Haselton, M. G., Nettle, D., and Andrews, P.W. (2005). "The evolution of cognitive bias. In D. M. Buss (Ed.), *Handbook of Evolutionary Psychology*, pp. 724-746.

Hoboken, Wiley.

Hackman, J. R. (2002). *Leading Teams: Setting the Stage for Great Performances*. Harvard Business School Press.

Hagstrom, W. O. (1964). "Traditional and modern forms of scientific teamwork". *Administrative Science Quarterly* 9(3): 241-263.

Hambrick, D. C., T. S. Cho and M. Chen. (1996). "The influence of top management team heterogeneity on firms' competitive moves". *Administrative Science Quarterly* 41(4): 659-684.

Hanks, G. F. (1995). "Excellence teams in action". *Management Accounting* (February): 33-36.

Hansen, M. T. (2009). "When internal collaboration is bad for your company". *Harvard Business Review* (April): 82-88.

Harrison, D. A., K. H. Price and M. P. Bell. (1998). "Beyond relational demography: Time and the effects of surface- and deep-level diversity on work group cohesion". *The Academy of Management Journal* 41(1): 96-107.

Harrison, D. A., K. H. Price, J. H. Gavin and A. T. Florey. (2002). "Time, teams, and task performance: Changing effects of surface- and deep-level diversity on group functioning". *The Academy of Management Journal* 45(5): 1029-1045.

Haas, M. R. (2006). "Knowledge gathering, team capabilities, and project performance in challenging work environments". *Management Science* (August): 1170-1184.

Heerema, D. L. and R. L. Rogers. (1991). "Is your cost accounting system benching your team players?" *Management Accounting* (September): 35, 38-40.

Hemp, P. (2003). "The DHL EuroCup: Shots on goal. *Harvard Business Review* (November): 43-52. (Figuring out how to foster corporate team building through intense competition).

Henderson, A. D. and J. W. Fredrickson. (2001). "Top management team coordination needs and the CEO pay gap: A competitive test of economic and behavioral views". *The Academy of Management Journal* 44(1): 96-117.

Herath, H. S. B., W. G. Bremser and J. G. Birnberg. (2010). "Facilitating a team culture: A collaborative balanced scorecard as an open reporting system". *Advances in Management Accounting* (18): 149-173.

Herrenkohl, R. C. (2004). *Becoming a Team: Achieving A Goal*. South-Western Educational Publishing.

Hertenstein, J. H. and M. B. Platt. (1998). "Why product development teams need management accountants". *Management Accounting* (April): 50-55.

Hill, L. A., G. Brandeau, E. T. Sal and K. Lineback. (2014). "Collective genius". *Harvard Business Review* (June): 94-102. (Smart leaders are rewriting the rules of innovation).

Hillmann, M. R., P. Dongier, R. P. Murgallis, M. Khosh, E. K. Allen and R. Evernham. (2005). "When failure isn't an option". *Harvard Business Review* (July/August): 41-50. (How teams consistently achieve the highest standards).

Hochbaum, D. S. and A. Levin. (2006). "Methodologies and algorithms for group-rankings decision". *Management Science* (September): 1394-1408.

Hollenbeck, J. R., D. R. Ilgen, J. A. LePine, J. A. Colquitt and J. Hedlund. (1998). "Extending the multilevel theory of team decision making: Effects of feedback and experience in hierarchical teams". *The Academy of Management Journal* 41(3): 269-282.

Holloman, C. R. and H. W. Hendrick. (1972). "Adequacy of group decisions as a function of the decision-making process". *The Academy of Management Journal* 15(2): 175-184.

Holloman, C. R. and H. W. Hendrick. (1972). "Effects of status and individual ability on group problem solving". *Decision Sciences* 3(4): 55-63.

Huckman, R. and B. Staats. (2013). "The hidden benefits of keeping teams intact". *Harvard Business Review* (December): 27-29..

Katz, R. (1982). "The effects of group longevity on project communication and performance". *Administrative Science Quarterly* 27(1): 81-104.

Katzenbach, J. R. and D. K. Smith. (1993). *The Wisdom of Teams: Creating the High Performance Organization*. Harvard Business School Press.

Katzenbach, J. R. and D. K. Smith. (2005). "The discipline of teams". *Harvard Business Review* (July/August): 162-171.

Kennedy, F. & Schleifer, L. (2007). "Team performance measurement: A system to balance innovation and empowerment with control". *Advances in Management Accounting* (16): 261-285.

Kirkman, B. L. and B. Rosen. (1999). "Beyond self-management: Antecedents and consequences of team empowerment". *The Academy of Management Journal* 42(1): 58-74.

Knight, D., C. C. Durham and E. A. Locke. (2001). "The relationship of team goals, incentives, and efficacy to strategic risk, tactical implementation, and performance". *The Academy of Management Journal* 44(2): 326-338.

Kunda, Z.(1990). "The Case for Motivated Reasoning". *Psychological Bulletin* Vol. 108, No. 3, 1990

Lancaster, K. A. and Strand, C. A. (2001). "Using the team-learning model in a managerial accounting class: An experiment in cooperative learning". *Issues In Accounting Education* (November): 549-567.

Lau, D. C. and J. K. Murnighan. (2005). "Interactions within groups and subgroups: The Effects of demographic faultlines". *The Academy of Management Journal* 48(4): 645-659.

Libby, T. and L. Thorne. (2009). "The influence of incentive structure on group performance in assembly lines and teams". *Behavioral Research In Accounting* 21(2): 57-72.

Limayem, M. (2005). Group decision support systems, in The Blackwell *Encyclopedia of Management: Management Information Systems*, Davis, G. B. (Ed.), *Blackwell Encyclopedia Of Management* Vol. 7. Blackwell Publishing, Malden, Massachusetts.

Louis, M. R. and J. M. Bartunek. (1992). "Insider/outsider research teams: Collaboration across diverse perspectives". *Journal of Management Inquiry*(June): 101-110.

Malone, T. W., R. Laubacher and C. Dellarocas. (2010). "The collective intelligence genome". *MIT Sloan Management Review* (Spring): 21-31.

Mankins, M., A. Bird and J. Root. (2013). "Making star teams out of star players: Here's how smart companies deploy their best people to get great results". *Harvard Business Review* (January/February): 74-78.

Mankins, M. C. (2004). "Stop wasting valuable time". *Harvard Business Review* (September): 58-65. (Seven techniques to help your management team make better and faster decisions).

Mathieu, J. E. and Schulze, W. (2006). "The influence of team knowledge and formal plans on episodic team process-performance relationships". *The Academy of Management Journal* 49(3): 605-619.

Maxwell, J. C. (2001). *The 17 Indisputable Laws Of Teamwork: Embrace Them and Empower Your Team.* Thomas Nelson.

Maxwell, J. C. (2006). The 17 *Essential Qualities of a Team Player: Becoming the Kind of Person Every Team Wants.* Thomas Nelson.

Maxwell, J. C. (2009). *Teamwork 101: What Every Leader Needs to Know*. Thomas Nelson.

McGrath, J. E. (1991). "Time, interaction, and performance (TIP): A theory of groups". *Small Group Research* (22): 147-174.

McNair, C. J. (1990). "Interdependence and control: Traditional vs. activity-based responsibility accounting". *Journal of Cost Management* (Summer): 15-23.

Miles, S. A. and M. D. Watkins. (2007). "The leadership team". *Harvard Business Review* (April): 90-98.

Mobrman, A.M., Mobrman, S. A. and Lawler, E. E. III. (1992). "The performance management of teams". In W. Bruns, Jr. ed. *Performance Measurement, Evaluation, and Incentives*. Boston: Harvard Business School Press: 217-241.

Montoya, M. M., Massey, A. P. and Lockwood, N. S. (2011). "3D collaborative virtual environments: Exploring the link between collaborative behaviors and team performance". *Decision Sciences* 42(2): 451-467.

Mullenweg, M. (2014). The CEO of Automatic on holding "auditions" to build a strong team. *Harvard Business Review* (April): 39-42.

Murtha, B. R., Challagalla, G. and Kohli, A. K.. (2011). "The threat from within: Account managers' concern about opportunism by their own team members". *Management Science* (September): 1580-1593.

Nayar, V. (2010). "A maverick CEO explains how he persuaded his team to leap into the future". *Harvard Business Review* (June): 110-113.

Needham, R.(2003). *Team Secrets Of The Navy Seals*. Andrews McMeel Publishing.

Neeley, T. (2015). "Global teams that work". *Harvard Business Review* (October): 74-81.

Nickerson, R. S.(1998). "Confirmation bias: A ubiquitous phenomenon in many guises". *Review of General Psychology*, 2, 1998.

Oakley, B., Felder, R. M., Brent R. and Elhajj, I. (2004). "Turning student groups into effective teams". *J. Student Centered Learning* 2(1): 9-34.

O'Leary-Kelly, A. M., Martocchio, J. and Frink, D. D. (1994). "A review of the influence of group goals on group performance". *The Academy of Management Journal* 37(5): 1285-1301.

Opdecam, E. and Everaert, P. (2012). "Improving student satisfaction in a first-year undergraduate accounting course by team learning". *Issues In Accounting Education* (February): 53-82.

Pentland, A. (2012). "The new science of building great teams". *Harvard Business Review* (April): 60-70.

Perlow, P. (2014)." Manage your team's collective time". *Harvard Business Review* (June): 23-25.

Perrow, C.,(1984). *Normal accidents: living with high-risk technologies*. Princeton University Press, Princeton, NJ.

Plous S.(1993). *The psychology of judgment and decision making*. New York, NY, McGraw-Hill, Inc.

Poole, M. S. and Hollingshead, Editors. A. B. (2004). *Theories of Small Groups: Interdisciplinary Perspectives*. Sage Publications.

Ready, D. A. and Truelove, E. (2011). "The power of collective ambition". *Harvard Business Review* (December): 94-102.

Reagans, R. and Zuckerman, E. W. (2001). "Networks, diversity, and productivity: The social capital of corporate R&D teams". *Organization Science*(12): 502-517.

Román, F. J. (2009). "An analysis of changes to a team-based incentive plan and its effects on productivity, product quality, and absenteeism". *Accounting, Organizations and Society* 34(5): 589-618.

Rothenberg, N. R.(2012). "The effect of imprecise information on incentives and team production". *Contemporary Accounting Research* 29(1): 176-190.

Ryan, K. (2012). "Gilt Groupe's CEO on building a team of A players". *Harvard Business Review* (January/February): 43-46.

Sarker, S., Sarker, S., Chatterjee, S. and Valacich, J. S. (2010). "Media effects on group collaboration: An empirical examination in an ethical decision-making context". *Decision Sciences* 41(4): 887-931.

Sarker, S., Kirkeby, S. and Chakraborty, S. (2011). "Path to "Stardom" in globally distributed hybrid teams: An examination of a knowledge-centered perspective using social network analysis". *Decision Sciences* 42(2): 339-370.

Schweer, M., Assimakopoulos, D., Cross, R. and Thomas, R. J. (2012). "Building a well-networked organization". *MIT Sloan Management Review*(Winter): 35-42.

Scofield, B. W. (2005). "Adapting cases for a team approach". *Journal of Accounting Education* 23(4): 248-263.

Siebdrat, F., Hoegl, M. and Ernst, H. (2009). "How to manage virtual teams". *MIT Sloan Management Review* (Summer): 63-68.

Sisco, R. (1992). "Put your money where your teams are". *Training* (July): 42-45.

Sosa, M. E., Eppinger, S. D. and Rowles, C. M. (2007). "Are your engineers talking to one another when they should?" *Harvard Business Review* (November): 133-136, 138, 140-142.

Sunstein, C. R. and Hastie, R. (2014). "Making dumb groups smarter. The new science of group decision making". *Harvard Business Review*(December): 90-98.

Tetlock, P.W.(1983). "Accountability and the perseverance of first impressions", *Social Psychology Quarterly*, 46(4).

The Cambridge Dictionary.

Tversky, A., $ Kahneman, D. (1974). "Judgment under Uncertainty: Heuristics and Biases". *Science*, New Series, 85, 1974.

Upton, D. R. (2009). "Implications of social value orientation and budget levels on group performance and performance variance". *Journal of Management Accounting Research* (21): 293-316.

Wagner, J. (1984). "Overcoming the we/they syndrome". *Management Accounting* (September): 47-50.

West, M. A. (2003). *Effective Teamwork: Practical Lessons from Organizational Research*. New Jersey: Blackwell Publishing.

Wilson E. B. (1962). An introduction to Scientific Research. New York, McGraw-Hill, 1952. *Wood F. G. Pitfall. Science*; 135, 1962.

Wilson, S. L. (2014). "Balance, teamwork part of vision for future". *Journal of Accountancy* (November): 62.

Wing, K. T. (2001). "Become a better leader". *Strategic Finance* (February): 65-68.

Wisner, P. S. (2001). "The impact of work teams on performance: A quasi-experimental field study". *Advances in Management Accounting* (10): 1-28.

Woolley, A. and Malone, T. (2011). "What makes a team smarter? Women". *Harvard Business Review* (June): 32-33.

Wright, P. (1993/1994). "Team Wilson: S Shingo award-winning approach to golf ball manufacturing excellence". *National Productivity Review*(Winter): 79-88.

www.Workforce.com

Young, M. and Selto, F. (1993)." Explaining cross-sectional workgroup performance differences in a JIT facility: A critical appraisal of a field based study". *Journal of Management Accounting Research* (5): 300-326.

Zellmer-Bruhn, M. and Gibson, C. (2006). "Multinational organization context: Implications for team learning and performance". *The Academy of Management Journal* 49(3): 501-518.

Made in the USA
Middletown, DE
13 July 2019